Language Interaction in
Teaching and Learning

Barbara Smith

Language Interaction in Teaching and Learning

by

LEE J. GRUENEWALD, Ph.D.
Director of Specialized Educational Services,
Madison Metropolitan School District

SARA A. POLLAK, M.A.
Language Consultant for Teacher Training;
formerly Supervisor, Speech, Language, and
Learning Disorders,
Madison Metropolitan School District

University Park Press
Baltimore

UNIVERSITY PARK PRESS
International Publishers in Medicine and Human Services
300 North Charles Street
Baltimore, Maryland 21201

Copyright © 1984 by University Park Press
Second printing, May 1984

Typeset by Maryland Composition Company, Inc.
Designed by Barry Goldman Designs, Baltimore
Manufactured in the United States of America by
The John D. Lucas Printing Company

Library of Congress Cataloging in Publication Data
Gruenewald, Lee J.
Language interaction in teaching and learning.

Includes index.
1. Students—Language. 2. Teachers—Language.
3. Interaction analysis in education. 4. Language and
education. 5. Education—Curricula. I. Pollak, Sara A.
II. Title.
LB1139.L3G775   1983   371.1'022   83-10621
ISBN 0-8391-1888-0

Contents

Preface

Speaking his language is the most complicated thing a human being does, and should he undertake to go even further and learn to read and write it, he multiplies one infinitude of complication by another. It is an awesome marvel that anyone can do any of these things, never mind do them well.[1]

To do them well is the reason for this book. To unravel the complications of language in learning is a great responsibility for teachers, and to do it well is an even greater burden.

This book attempts to help lighten the teachers' burden by developing a perspective enabling them to understand and become aware of the many facets of language which interact in curricula and instruction.

We are deeply grateful to Dr. Virginia Brown for her personal interest, thoughtful and insightful criticism, which steered our thinking to the needs of the classroom teacher. We extend our appreciation to the speech and language clinicians of the Madison Metropolitan School District, with particular thanks to Barbara Nyberg, Marianne Kellman, and Kathy Lyngass for their generosity in sharing materials and ideas. To Elaine Lohr and Lynn Conwell of the Madison Metropolitan School District, we extend our appreciation for their critical review.

[1] Mitchell, R. 1979. Less than words can say, In: The Underground Grammarian. Little, Brown and Co., Boston.

Language Interaction in
Teaching and Learning

Part *One*
Introducing The Process

Chapter *1*
Introduction

Language Interaction in Teaching and Learning is based on a federally funded project awarded to the authors in 1974. The objective of this project was to develop a training and demonstration program which would teach a process for modifying the learning problems of students. This process would entail the analysis of language interaction in instructional tasks. Since 1974, the authors have introduced the process in numerous workshops and consulting services in many school districts throughout the country. As a result of these experiences, the original manual has been expanded to reflect many teachers' requests for more information about developmental milestones of language as well as suggestions for intervention based on the analysis of language interaction.

During the last 10 years, there has been an explosion of information written for professionals on language development, disorders of language, strategies for assessment, and specific intervention techniques. Yet, teachers still experience difficulty integrating this information into their daily ongoing instructional tasks. This is because books and articles have not emphasized the relationship or interaction of language to daily ongoing instruction in the classroom. What has not been clearly understood and defined is the fact that a *continuous interaction between teacher, student, and concepts* exists in the teaching/learning process. This book provides essential information about language interaction which is applicable to teaching tasks in the classroom. Readers who desire to study the components involved in language interaction (content/concepts in the task, teacher language, and student language) in greater depth are encouraged to refer to the suggested readings at the end of Chapters 4, 5, and 6.

Many teachers assume that the cause of learning problems of students lies within the student. The teacher's intervention, therefore, automatically becomes student-centered. Although this may solve a temporary or situational problem, comprehensive intervention can take place only by analyzing the interaction that occurs between the student and the variables of the instructional task (classroom).

Classrooms must become natural language environments. Teachers must continue to grow in their understanding of language, language learning, successful language users, and how language users grow and develop (DeFord and Harste, 1982, p. 598).

This book limits the discussion of these variables to the language between student, teacher, and the concepts in the task.

The teacher is in the unique position of being able to observe a student's understanding and use of language in learning and to assess how failures take place. She or he is, therefore, the logical person to engage in the assessment and intervention of language interaction in the curriculum. A framework which will focus on this process of assessment is needed, particularly in mathematics and the reading content areas, within the classroom environment. The teacher should analyze not only the conceptual and linguistic skills that the child brings to the task but also the conceptual and linguistic skills that the task requires.

Scope and Sequence

This book is divided into three parts. Part I introduces the concept of the basic triad of language interaction. Part II provides an elaboration of each language component of the basic triad along with accompanying examples for analysis and implications for instruction. Part III features examples to help the teacher apply the process to areas of academic content. These examples and others provided throughout the book are taken from curricular materials as well as actual classroom activities that were taped by the authors in a variety of regular and special education classrooms.

For Whom Is This Book Intended?

This book is written primarily for regular and special education classroom teachers in preservice and in-service education.

The analysis of the interaction of language in academics will help the classroom teacher to modify potential learning problems before more serious problems develop. It is applicable to instructional programs for regular education students and handicapped students who are either integrated (mainstreamed) into regular classes or are receiving all or partial instruction in a self-contained special education classroom. In short, the analysis of language interaction is applicable to all teachers and students engaged in learning.

This teacher-centered approach does not contradict the professional responsibilities of related service personnel, such as speech and language clinicians and psychologists. On the contrary, it may enhance and stabilize the roles of these professionals. If the classroom teacher can increase his or her skills to include the analysis of language interaction in academic tasks, then the clinician can work more intensively with students who are handicapped in communication. Classroom teachers experiencing some difficulty in analyzing language interactions can consult the speech and language clinician or psychologist, who, in turn, could observe the student in specific tasks and guide the process of analysis and intervention. In the event that a learning problem related to the language interaction continues, the related service personnel would then have substantive information to proceed with a more formalized assessment and programming.

How To Use This Book

In preservice education, this book will apply to curriculum planning, courses in methods of instruction, and courses in assessment. For in-service education with professional staff, the process developed in this book can be incorporated into the school districts' ongoing staff development or in-service training in assessment and curriculum development.

The information presented is cumulative; therefore, the chapters must be read in the sequence presented. This approach will assist the reader in learning the process of analyzing language interaction in academics. In Part II, Language Analysis Guides are provided so that hypotheses can be formulated for intervention. These are specific analysis guides. Learning to use them will prepare the reader for the Summary Analysis of Language Interaction forms in Part III. These forms will only have meaning if the reader first understands and can use the Language Analysis Guides.

Finally, to learn this process demands that the reader develop a perspective that requires a different inner orientation to the analysis of learning problems. Although the reader may have some familiarity with each component of the triad, the interacting phenomena of these components requires a *different way of thinking* about the analysis of learning problems. This requires time, thought, and practice. The reader must have patience when assimilating the ideas set forth in this book so that the application and intervention will be successful.

Chapter *2*
Describing the Process

Purpose

Strategies

Definition of Language

Language in Context

All aspects of the classroom environment are important to the learning process, but the most crucial ingredient is language (Carroll, 1964; Cazden, 1972a; Lee and Rubin, 1979; Wilkinson, 1982). A special way of thinking about the important variables of language in the teaching/learning act must be stimulated. This will require that teachers look at the important language variables of teacher language, student language, and content/concepts in the instructional task from a different perspective than that which is customary. Most teachers may be familiar with these language variables and some of their effects on students' academic performances, but the teacher may *not* be familiar with how each language variable interacts with the others and the total impact of this interaction on the students' academic performances that results.

In addition to language, many important variables may affect the student's learning, i.e., curriculum materials; visual, auditory, and motor skills; teacher reinforcement; and student motivation.

Purpose

Descriptive information about the dynamic language interaction in instruction enables the teacher to prevent or modify students' learning problems. To describe this language interaction, instructional tasks in both curriculum and classroom are analyzed and hypotheses about the effect of the major language components in all learning are formulated.

Strategies

The following strategies are included in this process:

1. Identification and description of the interacting language components (content/concepts in the task, teacher language, and student language) of an instructional task

2. Discussion of developmental information about language and concepts in order to determine the congruence between the student's ability and teacher/curricular expectations

3. Description and analysis of the effect of the language components underlying instructional problems

4. Development of hypotheses (questioning) from the analysis of the language components in order to determine what language factor or factors need to be altered

5. Identification of possible intervention strategies the result from the hypotheses

This process of analyzing language interaction can be incorporated into an ongoing teaching program and will assist the teacher in developing an objective awareness of the language factors present in an instructional program. This descriptive process is applicable not only to teaching in the traditional content areas but also to the modification of curriculum for students enrolled in regular and special education classes. Developing this skill is an integral part of the teaching/learning process.

Language interaction is analyzed in *specific* instructional tasks. Most instructional personnel are familiar with this process, called task analysis, i.e., dividing a task into its smallest components in order to teach specific, discrete skills.

In the task analysis of language interaction, the emphasis is on language only and its interaction in the task.

To learn this process of assessment requires having skills in observation (knowing what to observe within the instructional task) and knowing what relevant questions to ask concerning the effect of language interaction on the student's academic performance. Rather than using formal standardized test results as the main source of information, the development of a descriptive process of learning skills of observation and analysis of the language factors should be used. At this initial level, standardized tests are not always useful in assessing the performance of a student because such tests do not reflect the dynamic effect of language.

Definition of Language

The study of language is so complex that it is difficult to learn and understand it in all of its ramifications. Teacher training has fostered the view of language as another subject with specific content rather than as a developmental process that allows the expression of concepts, reasoning, and abstract logic.

A necessary skill for assessing and modifying a student's learning performance is the awareness of linguistic and cognitive development and how this development relates to the expectations of academic task requirements.

Language is an acquired symbolic system. In order for the student to be a successful user of language, a set of requisites, suggested by Yoder and Miller (1972), must be met. For students to use language they must have:

1. Something to say (language content/concepts)

2. A way of saying it (syntax/rules)

3. A reason for saying it (pragmatics/use)

Bloom and Lahey (1978) suggested that:

Language can be defined in different ways by different persons for different purposes. A definition of language depends on the *context* in which one asks the question, *What is language?* (p. 1).

Here, the discussion of language is viewed as and limited to the *instructional context* of the classroom. Within this context, three interacting components of language are examined:

1. *Language content/concepts*: the use of concepts and operations which underlie all academic knowledge (can be represented in nonverbal and verbal forms)

2. *Teacher language*: the use of instructional language (the oral and written language of the teacher as well as the written language of the curriculum) to teach academic content

3. *Student language*: the acquisition, comprehension and use of language as a tool for acquiring academic knowledge and solving problems

Language in Context

Hymes (1972) stated that:

The key to understanding language in context is to start not with the language, but with the context. Only by viewing the relationship from the side of contexts can we see an essential part of what is going on when language is taught and used (p. xix).

This statement is consistent with the authors' view that language cannot be taught in a vacuum but is rather a continuously interacting phenomenon between speaker, listener, and environment. This interacting phenomenon of language is focused within the context of instruction in the classroom environment. The analysis of the effect of one language component upon a student's academic performance would only provide information on one part of the interaction. In order for the reader to understand the effect of the total interaction, information on each component is provided. The reader must realize, however, that the emphasis is on the analysis and application of the interacting effect of all three language components on student performance in the academic task.

Cazden (1972b) suggested that:

Because we all talk, we assume that we're experts on language. The trouble is that the knowledge of language we require as teachers is one level beyond using it ourselves, no matter how richly we may do so. We need to know more about language. And then we have to plan how to use that knowledge in the classroom (p. 2).

For example, words that are taken for granted, such as *more, less, before, after, all,* and *some,* very often have different meanings in different situations. Each meaning may be derived from the context in which the word is used. The student may be able to use such words appropriately in a conversational sense, but may not be able to use them appropriately in the instructional task in which he or she must solve a problem. For example, some words, like *first*, may have a spatial (*first* in line), temporal (*first* day), as well as quantitative meaning (*first* example). Language is present constantly in the classroom and is pervasive in all areas of academic as well as social interactions (Prutting, 1982).

A critical observer of language behavior, whether academic, social, or disordered, must understand that in each case, the language is different. The authors' concern is with the relevance of language in the task at hand (Halliday, 1973). The words *relevance* and *interaction* are basic to understanding and applying the descriptive process of language interaction in academics. If the function of assessment of language interaction is to aid in instructional decision making, the concept of relevance and interaction in instruction cannot be ignored.

Adelman (1971) felt that learning problems are based on a given student's success or failure as a function of the interaction between his or her strengths and weaknesses and specific classroom factors (context). In other words, learning problems result not only from the characteristics of the student but also from the characteristics of the classroom situation to which the student is assigned. Adelman (1971) further speculated that many students who encounter learning difficulties are referred for special classes because the regular classroom situation is not effectively personalized, i.e., individualized instruction. Adelman's premise should be taken a bit further to include other factors that may affect the regular learning environment and which indeed may be more crucial to it. These factors may include such things as teacher expectation, teacher language, teacher question-asking ability, the manner in which directions are presented, the matching of the teacher's language to the student's level of comprehension, and the conceptual and linguistic skills, which are brought by the student to the task or are required by the task. This is the interrelationship of language previously discussed. *Many students referred for testing may not have a specific disability; rather, the lan-*

guage interaction in the environment may be disabling.

The term *environment* (or as more recently referred to as *ecological*) *assessment* refers to a way of looking at students, taking into account the environment in which they operate and the interactions of the persons within that environment (Laten and Katz, 1975; Altwerger and Bird, 1982).

As Wiederholt et al. (1978) stated, many of the learning problems that students encounter may be a direct effect of the environment rather than of specific disabilities.

In summary, the environment is defined as the instructional task within the classroom, and the interaction is defined as the language interaction in this instructional task. This basic interaction will be described and explained in Chapter 3.

References

Adelman, H. 1971. The not-so-specific learning disability population. Except. Child. 37:349–54, January.

Altwerger, B., and Bird, L. 1982. Disabled: The learner or the curriculum. Top. Learn. Learn. Disabil. 1:69–78, January.

Bloom, L., and Lahey, M. 1978. Language Development and Language Disorders. New York: John Wiley and Sons, Inc.

Carroll, J. B. 1964. Language and Thought. Prentice-Hall, Inc., N.J.

Cazden, C. B. 1972a. Child Language and Education. Holt, Rinehart and Winston, Inc., New York.

Cazden, C. B., John, V. P., and Hymes, D., (eds.) 1972b. Functions of Language in the Classroom. Teachers College Press, New York.

DeFord, D., and Harste, J. 1982. Child language research and curriculum. Lang. Arts, 59:490–599, September.

Halliday, M. A. K. 1973. Explorations in the Function of Language. Butler and Tanner Ltd., Great Britain.

Hymes, D. 1972. In: C. G. Cazden, V. P. John, and D. Hymes (eds.), Functions of Language in the Classroom, Introduction. Teachers College Press, New York.

Laten, S., and Katz, G. 1975. A Theoretical Model for Assessment of Adolescents: The Ecological/Behavioral Approach. Madison Metropolitan School District, Madison, WI.

Lee, D. M., and Rubin, J. B. 1979. Children and Language, Reading and Writing, Talking and Listening. Wadsworth Publishing Co., Inc., Belmont, CA.

Prutting, C. 1982. Pragmatics as social competence. J. Speech Hear. Disabil., 47:123–133, May.

Wiederholt, L., Hammell, D., and Brown, V. 1978. The Resource Teacher: A Guide to Effective Practices. Allyn and Bacon, Inc., Boston.

Wilkinson, L. C. (ed.) 1982. Communicating in the Classroom. Academic Press, New York.

Yoder, D. E., and Miller, J. F. 1972. A Syntax Teaching Program. In J. E. McLean, D. E. Yoder, and R. L. Schiefelbusch (eds.), Language Intervention with the Retarded. University Park Press, Baltimore.

Chapter 3
The Triad

The total interaction of language affects both teaching and learning. This chapter introduces, describes, and illustrates the interactions of the basic triad.

GOALS

1. To introduce and describe the basic triad
2. To examine and illustrate each component of the basic triad (language content/concepts, teacher language, and student language)
3. To demonstrate the analysis of the language interaction involved in an instructional task

4. To demonstrate the formulation of hypotheses and intervention strategies, which are based on the analysis of the language interaction in the task
5. To introduce procedures for analysis and intervention

The Triad

Now that the process and strategies to analyze the language interaction have been presented (see Chapter 1), the next step is to explain the procedures necessary to carry out the process. These procedures will provide the foundation of the gestalt of the total interaction. Keep them in mind as each component is developed in the following three chapters.

Figure 3.1 shows the interaction of language, as represented in the basic triad (language content/concepts, teacher language, and student language), which is involved in all teaching. All components of the basic triad are present in instructional tasks. Although all of these components interact, the degree to which each one affects the student's success or failure in a task may vary.

Many teachers look at learning failures from only one part of the triad, i.e., student language. This may solve a temporary problem, but more comprehensive intervention can take place in the analysis of the interaction. Although teachers observe their students daily, their observations do not always include sufficient information about language. By becoming aware of the language

interaction within *specific instructional tasks*, teachers may be in a better position to prevent or modify learning difficulties. Teachers must continually ask questions about the extent to which learning difficulty is attributable to the student's lack of language competence for the task, the language used by the teacher, or the language content/concepts in the task. Other variables discussed in Chapter 1 enter into the instructional process; however, sufficient emphasis has not been given to how language *interacts* in a specific task.

Specific instructional tasks are derived from larger units of instruction. For example, teaching addition is the large instructional unit; single-column addition to 10 is the specific instructional task. If students do not succeed in small instructional tasks, the teacher may intervene by cuing, reteaching, or moving the student on to subsequent tasks in the anticipation that success will follow. For some students, this may seem to be the answer. For others, unsuccessful learning experiences in specific tasks may *signal* the beginning of learning problems with larger instructional units. Sometimes these signals are

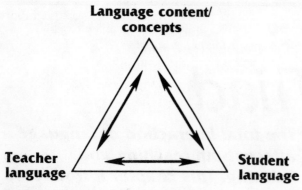

Figure 3.1 The interaction of language in the basic triad.

overlooked by the teacher. More important than repetition and completion of specific tasks is whether the students understand the principles involved and can transfer these principles to *new tasks* and *new situations* (problem solving). One way to assess whether the student has learned the principles is to analyze the language involved.

What Does the Teacher Need To Know about Language Content/Concepts in the Task?

The definition of language content is the meaning or substance of the words to be used in communication. This meaning depends on underlying concepts that are developed through experiences in the individual's environment. Time, space, and number are examples of concepts. They require operations such as the ability to classify, order, conserve, seriate, and do critical thinking, all of which are implicit in all academic tasks. Language content and concepts are linked because it is believed that within instructional tasks, the two are inextricably related.

Concept development underlies all academic learning—comprehension in reading, problem solving, and critical thinking in mathematics, social studies, and science. These concepts are expressed primarily through oral and written language and derive their meaning from the context in which they are used.

What Needs To Be Known about Teacher Language in the Task?

Teacher language may include written instructions and directions in curricular materials. The language used by the classroom teacher influences the responses of the students. For example, a student's inability to respond correctly to a teacher's direction may be caused not by the student's lack of knowledge but rather by inappropriate length, a rate of speech that is too rapid, or the use of multiple concept words in a direction.

Many teachers are not aware of how much talking they do and what its effect is on their students. They must know what their expectations are; otherwise, there will be a confusing cycle of questions in which the teacher asks an inappropriate question and obtains an inappropriate response, which leads to more teacher questions.

In curricular materials (instructional language), the use of multiple concepts in directions can cause problems for students. The student may understand one or two concepts but may not be able to remember or order all the concepts that are present in the direction.

Analyzing teacher language or curricular materials will assist the teacher in gaining insights into the patterns of language influence on the student. These insights will also help the teacher to revise his or her language behavior in order to maximize teaching strategies and obtain the desired academic goals.

What Needs To Be Known about Student Language in the Task?

Teachers need to listen not only to *what* the students are saying but also *how* they are saying it. In learning about the student's comprehension and use of language in instructional tasks, teachers cannot always rely on the tests of speech and language clinicians or on commercial tests of language performance. It is the teacher's responsibility to observe and understand the language performance of the student in *relevant* tasks in order to determine the following:

1. Whether the student has sufficient language to do the task

2. The level of language development (structure and content) of the student so that the teacher can use language at a level commensurate with that of the student

3. Whether the student has sufficient oral language to use written language (reading and writing)

What Needs To Be Known about Hypotheses?

The word *hypothesis* usually is used within a formal research paradigm. This book uses the term informally as a means of stimulating thinking about possible solutions to problems that occur in daily instruction.

A hypothesis is best defined as a question or implied question to be answered by collecting further information. Many persons do not state hypotheses as questions but rather as conclusions, inferences, assumptions, or statements of fact. The reader may develop hypotheses that are different from those developed by the authors. This is acceptable; there are many options. It is the process of developing and checking out hypotheses that is the crucial factor.

How is the Analysis of Language Interaction Incorporated into the Teaching Context?

A specific instructional task involving a math story problem in subtraction was selected because of 1) increasing concern by educators about the difficulty students experience in solving word and story problems; and 2) the implications of language interaction.

> *Teacher:* I have a story problem I want you to do. I will do it too. First, I want you to listen. Then, I will give you a copy of it and we will do it together and then we will do the figuring. The first thing we are going to do—I want to ask you to think whether or not you have to do addition or subtraction first. Don't just write down plus or minus. Just do the whole problem. Would you please put down your sign so I know exactly what you did?

Story problem

Yesterday Sue traveled 36 miles. Today Ed traveled 53 miles. How many more miles did Ed travel than Sue?

> *Teacher:* Okay, let's see. David, you said you plussed 36 and 53 and Debbie, you said you plussed also.

What were the key words in that story?

> *Debbie:* How many.
> *David:* How many more.
> *Teacher:* How many more. Does that tell you you had to be adding?
> *Both students:* Yes
> *Teacher:* We want to know how many miles. Are we going to put them together or find a difference? Ed traveled more miles. Right? When we are finding more miles are we adding or subtracting?
> *Students:* No response.

Usually, a teacher revises his or her strategy to reteach this task. Many teachers assume that additional drill in addition and subtraction, additional practice with key words, provision of more cuing, or providing better reinforcement will solve the problem. These strategies may solve a temporary problem of math computation. Indeed, the students may be able to perform the operation of subtraction. *What is at issue here is that the students are expected to perform subtraction within a word problem.* Because so much emphasis is placed on computation, the essential information concerning language in math is neglected.

Key words are being used to teach computation in word problems. This may be appropriate if the student understands the meaning of key words. For example, *how many* indicates addition; *how many more* can indicate addition or subtraction; and *how many more than* always refers to subtraction. However, even if students understand these key words, the question arises whether they understand them within the context of the story problem.

To determine the effect of language in this math problem, the teacher needs to obtain information about the three language components that comprise the basic triad. Administering a standardized test will not yield information as to *why* or *how* the student is experiencing difficulty related to the language interaction. The score on a test may encourage premature conclusions or inferences about the student's performance.

After information on the three language components of the triad is obtained, the next step is to formulate the hypotheses to be used in intervention.

What Does Analysis of the Language Components in the Math Example Reveal?

Language content/concepts:

1. The teacher's explanation and direction included concept words such as *first, together, figuring, adding, subtracting, plus, minus,* and *sign.*

2. Concept words in the word problem included *how many* and *how many more than.*

Teacher language:

1. Explanations and directions were too long.

2. Grammatical structure was confusing.

3. The teacher asked a series of three questions without a student response.

Student language:

1. There was not enough student language in the example to analyze whether the students could understand and use complex sentence forms.

2. The students did not understand the key words *how many* and *how many more* and the application of these words to the computation of the problem.

What Hypotheses Can Be Formulated from the Information Obtained on the Three Language Components?

Hypothesis 1 The student may understand that the concept words *how many* implied addition but may not understand that the words *how many more* implied subtraction (difference).

Hypothesis 2 The student may understand the key words but was not able to apply them when they are contained in a math sentence.

Hypothesis 3 The length and complexity of the direction and explanation may have prevented the students from understanding the problem.

Hypothesis 4 The series of three teacher questions, which attempted to clarify the concept of difference, may have confused the student.

Hypothesis 5 The teacher may not have had information to determine the level of the student's comprehension and use of vocabulary and sentence structure.

What Are the Implications for Instruction?

From the previous steps in this process, strategies for intervention can be planned. The hypotheses generated in all three parts of the triad must be taken into consideration. Based on knowledge of the student, the teacher should use some priorities in selecting the hypotheses for intervention. Two hypotheses that seem to significantly relate to the student's problem in the math task have been arbitrarily selected:

Hypothesis 1 Did the student understand that the concept words *how many* implied addition but not understand that the words *how many more* implied subtraction (difference)?

Through manipulative tasks, determine if the students understand the meaning of the words *how many* and *how many more.* All students benefit from manipulative experiences for gaining meaning or developing the concept.

Relate the meaning of addition (*how many*) and subtraction (*how many more*) to the words in the manipulative tasks.

After the students have acquired the meaning of the words *how many* and *how many more* to addition and subtraction, then apply the skill to story problems—first oral and then written.

Hypothesis 3 The length and complexity of the direction and explanation may have prevented the students from understanding the problem.

Reduce the length by modifying the language of the explanation and direction, as follows:

Teacher: I have a story problem that I want you to do. I will give you a copy of the story, and we will read it together. You must decide whether to add or subtract. Put down the correct sign and then do the whole problem.

The results of the analysis and intervention may lead to a solution of the students' problem in the specific task, or it may serve as a basis for further questioning.

This analysis and intervention was purposely constructed as a simple demonstration of the process in order to provide a basis for its application in the more complex academic tasks presented in Chapters 7 and 8.

What Are the Procedures for the Analysis of Language Interaction?

The development of procedures for analysis flow from the purpose, process, and strategies of the language interaction and is as follows:

Purpose   To provide descriptive information about the dynamic interaction in instruction

Process   To analyze instructional tasks in both curriculum and the classroom through the development of question strategies which address the major language components in learning

Strategies

1. Identification of the interacting language components;

2. Identification of the effect of the language components in instruction;

3. Description of developmental information related to the language components;

4. Development of questioning strategies (hypotheses formulation); and

5. Identification of possible intervention strategies.

The process and strategies are the framework for the analysis of language interaction. The procedures for this analysis will organize the teacher's observation and intervention. They are:

1. Selection of student or students

2. Collect information about the three interacting language components of the triad in a specific instructional task.

3. Formulate hypotheses concerning the effect of the language interaction.

4. Utilize these hypotheses to develop intervention strategies.

Procedures can be operationally defined by answering the questions *who, how,* and *when.*

Who

Who Is Selected?   An individual student or a group of students in regular or special education classes who exhibit repeated difficulty in a specific instructional task are selected.

Who Does the Analysis?   The initial observation and analysis are done by the regular and special education teachers in self-contained, resource and/or in integrated (mainstreamed) classes. Further analysis may include information from observations by other professionals, such as speech and language clinicians, who can assist the teacher in analyzing and interpreting the question and intervention strategies. If the student is referred for multidisciplinary assessment (or reassessment), the information concerning the language interaction in instructional tasks should be incorporated into the total assessment process.

How

How Is Information Collected?   Information is collected in the following ways:

1. Observation
2. Use of inventory forms (introduced in Part II); review and analysis of curriculum; taping (audio and video); and teachers' observations of each other

How Are Hypotheses Formulated?   Hypotheses must be based on a specific set of criteria as follows:

1. Information collected as discussed (hypotheses should follow from this information)

2. Appropriateness and relevancy (hypotheses should relate to specific task observed within academic context)

3. Distribution (should be hypotheses about each of the three components of triad)

4. Form (hypotheses should involve "something to be found out," not statement of fact)

It is extremely important to ask questions continually about all three interacting parts of the triad so that *comprehensive* intervention can take place.

How Are Intervention Strategies Developed? The hypotheses in each part of the triad form the basis for the intervention. Test out these hypotheses by modifying:

1. Teacher language (speaking mode, grammatical mode, and instructional mode)

2. Language content/concepts (in task, in teacher language, and in student language)

3. Student language (structure, semantics, and pragmatics)

Use developmental information regarding language and concepts to determine at what level intervention should take place.

When

When Does the Teacher Engage in This Process? The teacher engages in this process:

1. When the student or students exhibit repeated learning problems in a task in spite of teacher cuing and reteaching

2. Before considering the referral of selected students to a multidisciplinary team (which may eliminate the need for some of the referrals)

3. In planning curricular units, to determine whether there may be a match/mismatch between curricular expectations and the student's level of development

When Is This Process Terminated? The process of hypotheses formulation and intervention is ongoing and will eventually be assimilated into the teaching skills. However, the analysis of specific instructional tasks terminates when the intervention is successful. The same student, however, may experience a learning problem in a different instructional task, at which point the analysis is repeated. This means that the teacher is constantly assessing the effect of the language interaction from task to task whenever learning problems occur.

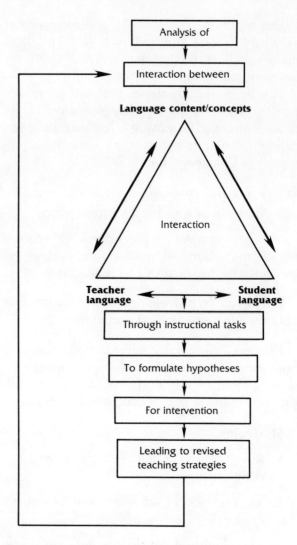

Figure 3.2 A flow chart of the analysis of language interaction.

An analysis of the interaction between language content/concepts, teacher language, and student language described in this chapter can best be summarized in a flow chart (see Figure 3.2).

The Expanded Triad

The expanded triad (see Figure 3.3) encompasses the many interactions *within* and *between* each language component of the basic triad. The three smaller triads are included within the basic triad in order to emphasize that they are always a part of the whole. These smaller triads will be separated for elaboration in Chapters 3, 4, and 5.

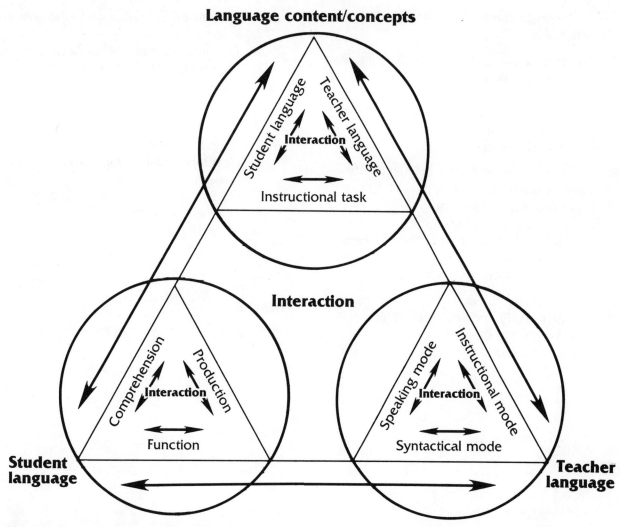

Figure 3.3 The expanded triad.

Review Questions

Circle the correct answers

1. In this chapter, hypotheses formulation is based upon:
   a. Impressions
   b. Assumptions
   c. Observation data
   d. All of the above

2. This process is designed to help you:
   a. To identify children with language disorders
   b. To observe and analyze language behavior in all children
   c. To analyze language interaction with a target child in an academic task
   d. To identify children with language problems through formalized testing

3. The assessment of language interaction in instruction will help to reveal:
   a. What to teach in the language arts curriculum
   b. Whether a student should be placed in a special language program
   c. Some reasons which may underlie the student's failure to perform the task
   d. Whether the student has a visual/motor problem

4. This chapter views language assessment in the academics as:
   a. Primarily concept-oriented
   b. The interacting process of student language, teacher language, and language content/concepts in the task
   c. Primarily teacher questions and directions

d. The assessment of semantic comprehension

5. The *initial* analysis of language interaction in a specific task is done by the:
   a. Psychologist
   b. Speech and language clinician
   c. Special education teacher
   d. Classroom teacher

6. The process of assessing language interaction in academic tasks is:
   a. An ongoing assessment
   b. An integral part of teaching
   c. A method of organizing the teachers' observations
   d. All of the above

7. The language used by the classroom teacher directly and indirectly affects the responses of the student.
   _____True   _____False

8. The key to the assessment of language interaction is:
   a. The utilization of standardized tests
   b. Observing a student in isolation
   c. Drawing conclusions based on one example
   d. None of the above

9. Ecological assessment includes:
   a. Developmental information on language
   b. Student interaction with environment
   c. Teachers' expectations
   d. All of the above

Answers

1. c; 2. c; 3. c; 4. b; 5. c, d; 6. d; 7. true; 8. d; and 9. d

Part *Two*
Elaborating the Process

Chapter 4
Language Content/ Concepts

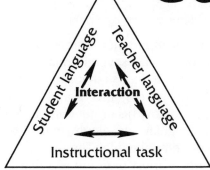

Student language / Teacher language

Interaction

Instructional task

Language content/concepts underlie the learning of all academic tasks. This chapter focuses on the identification and analysis of important concepts and operations in specific instruction. Implications for instruction for each concept are also provided.

GOALS

1. To introduce information about concepts, operations, and skills and how they relate to instructional learning
2. To introduce information about concept development

3. To demonstrate the analysis of language content/concepts in instructional tasks
4. To discuss implications for instruction
5. To provide an inventory for recording language content/concepts

In order to use language as a meaningful tool for learning, a student must have *something to say*. This something to say is the *language content (semantics)*. The meaning of language content depends on the student's cognitive development (Bloom, 1978), which can be regarded as the process of learning and knowing (Kean and Personke, 1976; Smith, 1983). This development involves such concepts as time, space, and number, all of which are abstract ideas generalized from concrete experiences. The development of these concepts requires operations and skills, such as the ability to classify, order, conserve, seriate, and do critical thinking. These concepts, operations, and skills are *implicit* in all academic tasks; they are made *explicit* through the use of language. The terms *language content* and *concepts* are linked because they cannot be separated within a learning task.

The teacher must be aware of the difference between the *implicit* and *explicit* skills that are inherent in instructional tasks. Explicit use refers to the concept words, or vocabulary, whereas implicit use refers to underlying concept/operations, such as classification, seriation, causality, and critical thinking. For example, the vocabulary for addition includes *adding, plussing, numeral,* and *sum* and represents the *explicit* use of language; the *implicit* skills required for addition would be *grouping, seriation, conservation,* and *one-to-one correspondence*.

To further demonstrate this point in an instructional task, consider the following example from a reading comprehension test (McGuire and Bumpus, 1971, p. 29, Form X):

> The children saw three birds in the tree yesterday. But now there were only two. The mother bird was flying near the ground. She kept chirping loudly.

Questions

1. The main problem in this story is:
   a. What kind of birds were in the nest?
   b. Where was the bird's nest?
   c. Where was the other baby bird?
   d. What color were the eggs?

2. Probably the baby bird had:
   a. Gone to look for worms
   b. Flown to the next tree
   c. Played hide and seek
   d. Fallen out of the nest

3. One thing that is not important to know in solving this problem is:
   a. The children had seen three birds
   b. The mother bird was chirping loudly
   c. The mother bird was flying near the ground
   d. The children liked to watch the birds

In order to accomplish successful ongoing assessment/intervention, strategies are needed for analyzing whether the student has the implicit concepts/operations and explicit concept words (vocabulary) to accomplish the instructional task. This is illustrated for the given example as follows:

Implicit Concepts/Operations

Question 1 Classification (item exclusion): student required to eliminate those items that are not the main problem

Question 2 Temporality (time): student required to comprehend the temporal concept of past tense; inference student required to hypothesize outcome

Question 3 Classification (item exclusion)

Explicit Vocabulary

Question 1 Main problem

Question 2 Gone, flown, played, fallen, probably

Question 3 Not important to know

The literature in the field of cognition and concept learning is voluminous. *Discussion will focus only on what is applicable and relevant to the process of language assessment and intervention in academic subjects.*

The development of language and cognition are intertwined. Although there can be cognition without language, as in handicapping conditions such as hearing impairment and retardation, communication and learning is limited (Bloom, 1978; Inhelder and Piaget, 1964; Rice, 1980). A student's use of language reflects his or her level of cognitive functioning. Carroll (1977) reinforced this notion when he stated:

> To comprehend language is to comprehend the concepts, propositions, inferences, qualification . . . and anything else that is expressed in language, either spoken or written (p. 1).

This view has important considerations in teaching moderately and severely retarded students. If the retarded student's language ability approximates his or her cognitive ability and both are significantly below his or her chronological age, then the regular developmental progression would not be applicable. The teacher of the retarded student must present tasks that are functional and appropriate for the student's chronological age but are also at his or her cognitive developmental level. For example, a student with a chronological age of 13 who has a cognitive developmental and language stage of age 4 might be presented with a task of sorting bath and hand towels. This, rather than sorting blocks, would be a functional activity.

The discussion on the analyses of cognitive skills is based on precepts developed by Piaget, who provided a systematic description of the processes by which children acquire knowledge (Schwebel and Raph, 1973). Piaget was not concerned with the specific age at which children acquire skills but rather with the process and sequence in which they are developed. Piaget and his followers believed that the stages of sequential cognitive development are invariant, but that the rate of development varies. They also believed that the earliest stages in the sequence are prerequisite for later stages. Researchers disagree about the invariance and sequential stages but on the whole, Piaget's stages of cognitive development are widely used as a framework for observing the development of children. These are not discrete stages; rather they form a progression, indicating change.

The following are the Piaget stages of cognitive development:

1. *Sensorimotor stage (birth–2 years of age)* The child learns about his or her environment through his or her senses and

motor responses. Meaningful use of language is a clue that he or she is ready to pass to the next stage.

2. *Preoperational stage (early: 2–4 years of age; late: 4–7 or 8 years of age)* The major characteristic of the early preoperations stage is that the child develops a symbolic function and language system but is bound to the "here and now." This means that he or she does not have the ability to deal with cause and effect. Progressing to the later preoperational period, the child uses language to form generalizations and develop inferential thinking, becoming less bound to the immediate events in the environment. The major sentence structures and their constituents become fully developed.

3. *Concrete operational stage (7–11 or 12 years of age)* The child uses language to develop skills for concrete logical thinking. Operational skills that develop include the ability to take another person's point of view and the ability to conserve, reverse, or manipulate higher levels of classification.

4. *Formal operational stage (12 years of age–adulthood)* Language is used at its highest level to express abstract thoughts and combinations of symbolic logic. The child also develops the ability to hypothesize and evaluate the consequences of his or her actions.

The following concepts and skills are described and analyzed within the context of instructional tasks:

1. Classification

2. Conservation

3. Time

4. Seriation

5. Space

6. Causality

7. Critical thinking

Each section discusses the concept, present developmental data, concept words (vocabulary), and implications for instruction.

The cognitive checklists that follow these sections provide developmental information by stage and chronological age. Each checklist serves as a reference to show: 1) the incremental progression within the concept area; 2) whether the student has attained the earlier conceptual requisites for the task; and 3) whether the conceptual requisites for the instructional task are beyond the student's development level and may account for his or her failure in the task. The teacher may want to refer to this information when developing hypotheses for intervention.

Classification

The operations of classification is a strategy for organization and is present in all academic and nonacademic activities. Unless a student has classification skills, he or she will not be able to process and retain all the information received through the senses.

Initially, students must have experiences with the operations of sorting or grouping, combining, and ordering familiar objects within his or her environment on the basis of *similarities* and *differences*. A student usually starts forming combinations by collecting toy animals in a box, for example, and proceeds further by separating them into sheep, horses, cows, etc. He or she can do this with color, property, size, or function. The student begins with the likeness of one thing to another and distinguishes it as different from other things. These same objects can be regrouped or reclassified, depending upon what properties the student is judging to be the same.

> Piaget distinguishes grouping as the principle from which stem classification, seriation, conservation, number, and space understanding (Schwebel and Raph, 1973, p. 26).

As the student learns sameness, he or she must learn *negatives* to express complementary classes, for example, trucks and things to ride in versus *not* trucks. For every item that belongs in a class, there are items that do not; it is necessary for the student to comprehend that in putting all red objects together, all objects that are *not* red must be eliminated. It is often assumed that because a student knows sameness among objects he or she also knows the differences.

There are two interrelated systems of classifications. One is nonnumerical, which is used to establish relationships in providing a framework for logical thinking; the other involves numerical experiences, which lead to the idea of sets. As a result of this process, number sequences develop. A set is defined as a "collection of any kind of things belonging together" (Williams and Shuard, 1970, p. 30). Sets can be put together into a whole as well as separated into parts. This is a precursor of *addition, subtraction,* and *comparison*. This activity involves sequencing as well as the important language concepts of *all, some, more, less, enough, next to, before,* and *after*.

Classification requires the ability to manipulate, order, group, and transform verbal symbols, both on a receptive and expressive basis. This is a prerequisite for forming new classes, retaining information, and transmitting information from one person to another. Classification skills are present in all academic tasks (Gruenewald, 1972).

Development

There are three developmental levels of classification behavior:

1. *Perceptual* Children below 5 years of age tend to select a perceptual or descriptive attribute of shape, color, size, etc.

2. *Functional* Older children most often select attributes based on a functional or relational quality (to cook with, to hear with, happy, sad).

3. *Categorical* After 8 years of age, children tend to form groups based on generic or class names (animals, fruit, vehicles).

Inhelder and Piaget (1964) delineated four major stages in classification learning.

Stage 1—Graphic Collections (about 2½–5 Years of Age) The child arranges objects randomly. At this stage, the child groups objects without any specific criterion. He or she can think of only one or two elements at a time.

Stage 2—Nongraphic Collections (about 4–7 Years of Age) The child sorts objects on a perceptual level, for example, the color blue. Although the child at this stage may group or make meaningful collections, he or she is not able to perform class inclusion (all items belonging together based on a single or multiple criterion).

According to Inhelder and Piaget (1964), true classification demands more than perceptual judgments; it demands mental operations. *The child must not only take in information, but must also remake information.*

Stage 3—Class Inclusion All items belonging together based on a single or multiple criterion are classified. This is the defining characteristic of this stage. According to Kamii and Peper (1969), this is classification.

An example of class inclusion would be as follows: "Put all the objects in the box that could take you places." The array of objects in front of the child would include a car, truck, horse, chair, airplane, cow, and boat.

Multiple classification refers to the ability to group objects into various subgroups. Objects can be rearranged and regrouped depending on the specific criterion. For example, a leather belt can be grouped into 1) clothing; 2) leather goods; or 3) fasteners. Multiple classification demonstrates that classes are not fixed or permanent.

Stage 4—Period of Formal Operations Class inclusion and multiple classification are prerequisites for the attainment of formal operations in adolescence (Kamii and Peper, 1969). Concrete operations (classification) structure only the concrete empirical data; formal operations represent reasoning with the structures that are achieved in the period of concrete operations. The adolescent begins to reason with categories and tests and verifies his or her hypotheses.

Concept Words (Vocabulary)

It is not feasible to list specific vocabulary here. The vocabulary of classification is generated by the requirements of the task. For example:

Perceptual—words denoting color, shape, size, texture, form

Functional—words denoting use, relationship

Categorical—words denoting class name

Implications for Instruction

The importance of classification as part of the total language system is based on the observation of many students who had difficulty putting thoughts into words, sequencing ideas, or stating reasons for actions. Students may not have sufficient experience in giving precise descriptions of objects, pictures, or events and in giving logical explanations of actions. Classification tasks are intended to develop these skills; however, students may acquire deficiencies in classification skills at an early age because of teachers' misperceptions of the requirements of a task. Teachers often confuse the task of sorting and classifying. Many early elementary reading and math activities include exercises in classification that are in reality visual and auditory discrimination exercises (sorting). A student may sort objects along various dimensions such as size, color, or shape, usually referred to as *attributes*. Therefore, a teacher may say to a student, "Put all the blue blocks in this pile and red blocks in that pile." What is happening, however, is that the student is making a visual discrimination based on color. In order to determine whether a student is classifying, the teacher must ask questions that will elicit appropriate responses such as, "Show me which ones belong together," or "Show me which ones do *not* belong together." After the student has grouped the series of objects in any fashion, the important question that must be asked is, "Why do these go together?" The student must be able to demonstrate that he or she can group according to one or more attributes, i.e., size, shape, color, etc. Then the student must be able to verbalize his or her decision for the grouping. He or she may understand the concept, *but until he or she uses language to express it, progression to more abstract tasks will not be possible.*

Teachers may also assume incorrectly that because a student uses categorical terms such as animals, clothing, or fruit, he or she is able to classify. However, the student may not understand the attributes that are used to make these categorical classifications. For example, a student may group sheep, cows, and dogs as animals but not be able to give a reason for the grouping, such as four legs, tail, etc.

A teacher may misjudge the ability of a student to classify because his or her response did not meet the teacher's expectation of the instructional task. For instance, to check whether the students were learning the operation of classifying by using the concepts of *big* and *little*, a teacher gave the following direction:

> Here are some sponges. Put them into two groups.

Her expectation was for the students to demonstrate knowledge of classification by grouping big sponges into one group and little sponges in a second group. This task had been practiced the previous day. One boy squeezed each sponge and put both big and little sponges into each of the two groups. The teacher regarded this response as incorrect because it did not meet her expectation of grouping by *big* and *little* sponges. What she had indeed asked for was to sort the sponges into two groups. She did not realize that the student was grouping correctly, but that the attributes he had selected were that of *hard* and *soft* (as demonstrated by his squeezing techniques). The student was able to classify at the perceptual level of texture rather than of size.

Evidence indicates that children who are mentally retarded, hearing-impaired, learning-disabled, language-delayed or otherwise handicapped demonstrate inadequacies in the development of classification skills. Because this development includes all of the concepts discussed in this chapter, the teacher (regular or special education) will benefit from the developmental information presented in each checklist.

Classification skills are embedded in the following academic areas (Kellman and Nyberg, 1980):

Mathematics
Formation of sets
Math operations
Story problems

Social studies
Outlining
Historical concepts (i.e. major issues of World War II)
Geography (class inclusion: home, city, county, state, country, hemisphere)

Language arts
Reading (grouping of letters to make words; combining small syllables to make larger words)
Reading comprehension (main ideas, part/ whole relationships)
Synonyms, antonyms, humor, and idioms

Science
  Classes of plants and animals
  Classes of nonliving things

Problem solving

Creative thinking

Conservation

Conservation can be defined as:

. . . the ability to realize that certain attributes of an object are constant, even though it changes in appearance (Pulaski, 1971, p. 242).

For example, pouring liquid from a tall, thin glass into a short, fat glass may change the appearance but not the volume; or the number of objects in a set remains the same, regardless of how the objects are arranged or combined. Nothing has been added or taken away in either example.

The ability to conserve is basic to the understanding of number, measurement, and space. It requires the child to physically and mentally act upon an object. Conservation appears during the late preoperational and concrete periods. Inherent in the ability to conserve is the ability of reversibility, which develops when the child is 5–8 years of age. The child will be able to conserve when he or she is no longer bound to sensory experiences and can begin to use logic.

Development

The ability to conserve develops at different times with different concepts:

Type	Approximate age of appearance
Number	5–7
Quantity	5–7
Length	7
Area	7–8
Time	8–9
Weight	9–10
Volume	11–12

Concept Words (Vocabulary)

Conservation vocabulary includes the following terms:

Number—*more, less, the same as, all, half, whole, few, before, after*

Size—*tall, short, skinny, fat, wide, narrow, high, low*

Area—*line them up the same way, some other way, before, after, the same as, more, not as much as*

Length—*taller than, higher than, shorter than, the same length as, on top of, under, alongside of, near, close to, up against*

Volume—*empty, full, more, less, too much, too little, all gone*

Weight—*heavy, light*

Time—*fast, slow, farther, older, younger*

Implications for Instruction

Many teachers find that first-grade students have difficulty with addition in a task that requires not only $4 + 1 = 5$ but also $1 + \square = 5$. The latter computation requires the ability to conserve and reverse thought. Copeland (1974a) suggested that a student has achieved reversibility when:

. . . one of two equal sets is rearranged . . . and he realizes that the number of each set has not changed" (p. 90).

Teachers must question whether first-grade children who are presented with a math problem similar to the given example can reverse thought.

The implication of conservation and reversibility also exists in language development. Passive voice, which is a difficult sentence construction for young children, requires the use of reversibility from the active voice, for example, "John hit the ball (active voice) and "The ball was hit by John" (passive voice). Questions are another example of reversibility (subject/verb), i.e., "Is John going home?" as contrasted with "John is going home."

Unless a student can conserve, he or she will have difficulty either adding or subtracting. For instance, a direction might be as follows:

Rename the 10s in 23

Take one 10 → make 10 ones

10s	ones	→	10s	ones
2	3		$\frac{1}{2}$	$\frac{1 3}{3}$

This direction requires the following skills:

1. Understanding equivalency, i.e., one 10 equals 10 ones

2. Understanding that the quantity concept does not change; 10 is still 10, regardless of how it is displayed; reducing two 10s to one and increasing three ones to 13 still does not change the total quantity

3. Understanding the concept of reversibility, which is inherent in this process

If the student has difficulty in this task, one of the first things the teacher needs to do is to be certain that the student has one-to-one correspondence. Second, conservation must be established. For instance, give the student 23 sticks and have him or her arrange them first in piles of twos, then in fives and 10s, each time counting the total number, regardless of the arrangement. The student must understand that each time, there will be a *remainder*. Third, have the student count and record the number of 10s and the number of ones. Then transfer one pile of 10s to the three ones and count the 10s and ones. Have the student count the total.

The teacher must be aware that the concept operations of conservation occur in many other subject areas in addition to math. In social studies, for example, the student must understand that although people may exist in different cultures at different times, they are still people; or in science, changes can occur within a classification system (phylum) without the class being changed.

Time

Temporal concepts can be expressed in two ways: temporal order (sequence) and duration (the interval between two events). A student should understand that the measurement of time is based on the existence of motion that can be time (Copeland, 1974b). In order for a student to be able to become operational with respect to time, he or she must be able to coordinate order and duration. The ability to order and perceive intervals is not completed until about 9 years of age.

There are many misconceptions about teaching time, which is often done in a mechanical, perceptual manner without developing an un-

derstanding of the underlying concepts and skills. This is especially true for calendar time, which is the traditional activity at the beginning of the day for young elementary-age students. The utility of this opening activity is questionable because on the whole, it is a rote activity and therefore not meaningful. Many of the concepts and vocabulary used in this task are not yet within the cognitive developmental level of the student. In some schools, this task is also customarily taught to young children who are hearing impaired or show varying degrees of retardation. Student failure can be incurred if tasks are presented to the student before he or she has the developmental ability to do them.

Development

Temporal behavior develops in five stages (Elkind and Flavell, 1969):

Stage 1—Concepts of Time Based on Order Time relates to the personal aspects of *before* and *after* without capacity of employing calendar or clock concepts. The child does not differentiate time from space or speed. *Faster* means *more time.*

Stage 2—Notion of Velocity or Speed Develops (Kindergarten or First Grade) Speed is a more fundamental notion than time. The child does not have reversibility yet and uses sequence order.

Stage 3—Ideas of Time, Distance, and Speed Coordinated (6–8 Years of Age) The child answers on a logical rather than perceptual basis. He or she understands the succession of events in time and duration in conservation of age differences (Copeland, 1974b).

Before a child can be expected to deal logically with telling time in terms of minutes, seconds, days, etc., he must attain the developmental stage of concrete operations (7–8 years of age) . . . At this stage, the ability to do reversible thinking, the ability to deal with seriated relationships is present in the child. At this stage, children also understand transitive relationships, such as "if $A = B$ and $B = C$, then it follows that $A = C$" . . . In this example, B is the middle term that established the relationship between A and AC. A clock is the middle term when used to establish the time relationship between two events. For example, two runners compare themselves to one another through the intermediary of a clock. Bob ran a mile in 5 minutes; George ran it in 6 minutes. Bob took less time than George.

Stage 4—Speed of Movement Can Be Separated from a Distance Traveled over Time
The child understands that the hour hand moving over a short distance is measuring the same time as the minute hand, which moves over a greater distance.

Stage 5—Historical Perspective Understood (Adolescence)
The child responds to time words before he or she uses them. Temporal concepts at the preschool level are primarily related to the personal aspects of *before* and *after* without the capacity of employing calendar and clock concepts.

Temporal skill	Years of age
Understands the following words	
today	2
tomorrow	2½
yesterday	3
Recognizes a special day of the week, such as Sunday	4
Uses words *yesterday* and *tomorrow* correctly	5
Tells whether it is morning or afternoon	5
Indicates the day of the week	6
Indicates the month	7
Indicates the season	7–8
Indicates the year	8
Indicates the day of the month	8–9
Is interested in historical time	9–10
Estimates duration of a conversation	12
Gives the time within 20 minutes	12
Has ability to tell which of two events in historical time occurred earlier or later	12
Understands B.C./A.D.	12 +
Constructs a time line of historical time	12 +

Concept Words (Vocabulary)

The following words are used to express time units:

Order (succession)	Duration
first, second, third, etc.	*morning*
before	*afternoon*
during	*evening*
after	*daytime*
since	*nighttime*
while	*old*
at the same time	*long time*
next	*today*
last	*tomorrow*
one more time	*yesterday*
and	*hour*
earlier	*day*
later	*young*
a while ago	*a little while*
now	*week*
then	*day*
	month
	year
	long
	short time
	long time

Implications for Instruction

If teachers want to ensure successful learning for their students, they need to examine their curricular materials to determine whether the student has the prerequisite understanding or developmental readiness for the task. They can then more easily adapt the materials to the student's cognitive and language level.

Temporal concepts are found in the following academic areas:

Social studies
  Dates
  Historical time

Language arts
  Time setting of the reading
  Selection of events
  Order of events

Mathematics
  Measurement

Science
  Motion
  Seasons
  Changes over time

The following math problem, for example focuses on measurement.

A turkey is to be cooked *20 minutes* for each pound. If a turkey weighing 10 pounds is to be done at *5 p.m.*, what *time* should it be put in the oven to cook?

The explicit vocabulary representing the temporal concepts in this example are *5 p.m.* and *20 minutes*. The underlying temporal concepts and operations (implicit) include:

1. Duration of time—Length of cooking time (20 minutes × 10)

2. Minutes to the hour (200 minutes ÷ 60 = $3\frac{1}{3}$ hours)

3. Reversibility (working backward from 5 p.m. to 1:40 p.m.)

According to Carpenter et al. (1981), problems involving time duration are difficult. He said:

> Fewer than a third of the 9-year-olds could find the time 8 hours after a given time or find the amount of time between 2 given hours of the day (p. 92).

This difficulty in manipulating time generates the following hypotheses:

Hypothesis 1 Does the student understand the concepts a.m. and p.m. as equivalent to morning, afternoon, or evening? In other words, does the student have the concept of a day?

Hypothesis 2 Does the student have the concept of hours and minutes within the hour?

Hypothesis 3 Does the student have the concept of duration as being equivalent to the interval between two points?

Hypothesis 4 Does the student have the ability to reverse an operation, i.e., go backwards in time from a given point?

Teachers must consider the temporal concepts included in the many tasks that students are required to do:

1. Order events chronologically

2. Recognize that stories and activities have a beginning and an end

3. Develop the notion that time involves co-ordination of speeds

4. Develop the concept of age

5. Recognize the part/whole relationship of time

6. Develop the understanding of *before* and *after*, which is necessary to sequence events in a logical order

Seriation

Another operation that the student needs to organize in his or her environment is learning the relationships between objects and putting them in order. This is seriation. As the student acquires the ability to seriate, a profound change in the quality of thinking can be observed (Voyat, 1973). According to Copeland (1974a), young children at the sensorimotor level seem to order objects through a trial-and-error procedure. To truly seriate requires the reversibility of thought and transitivity that occurs around 7–8 years of age.

As discussed in the section on conservation, reversibility of thought refers to the ability of the student to perceive order from more than one direction. This operation can be expanded to include reversing order in increasing and decreasing sizes, heights, gradation of colors and textures and qualities.

Problems that kindergarten and first-grade children have with ordinal and cardinal numbers may be based on their lack of this development of reversibility.

Transitivity can be defined as the coordination of a series of relations (Copeland, 1974a). This means that if the first item of a series is related to a second and a second item to a third, then the first item is related to a third. For example, if *B* is greater than *A* and *C* is greater than *B*, then *C* is also greater than *A*. This can be translated into: "If Mary is taller than John and Bill is taller than Mary, then Bill is also taller than John." It follows that Bill is the tallest.

Development

There are four stages in the development of seriation:

Stage 1 (Early Preoperational Period) True seriation is not actually occurring. The child pairs items according to whether they are big or little. He or she cannot use seriation in a constructive sense. By 3 or 4 years of age, the child begins to make arrays of two or three objects when seven objects are presented.

Stage 2 (Late Preoperational Period) The child, according to Piaget, has one-to-one correspondence. He or she can seriate 10 items and be able to use different materials. The child still uses a trial-and-error approach for solving seriation problems.

Stage 3 (Concrete Operational Period) The child has a strategy for solving the seriation problem that does not depend on trial and error.

> The ability to seriate or order, such as from the smallest to the largest, or to count at the operational level, that is, with true understanding of the inclusion relation involved, develops usually at seven or eight years of age. (Copeland, 1974a)

Stage 4 (Formal Operational Period) The child is able to represent how an ordered group will look before ordering the objects physically. He or she can also understand transitive relationships.

Concept Words (Vocabulary)

Some vocabulary associated with seriation are:

Number—ordinal (*first, second, third,* etc.)

Size—*big, bigger, biggest*

Length—*long, longer, longest*

Height—*tall, taller, tallest*

Space/time—*in front of, behind, before, after*

Amount—*least, most*

Implications for Instruction

Seriation is included in all subject areas. Teachers may not always be aware that a reading task such as, "Number the pictures according to the sequential episodes and then use as a reference for retelling the story," requires (1) the understanding of the part/whole relationships; (2) comprehension of the story; (3) the ability to use complex sentence structure; and (4) the ability to seriate. The teacher should question whether the student has the concepts of *before* and *after; first, second, third* (cardinal); *one, two,*

three (ordinal); and the sequential order of the parts to form a whole (logical ordering).

Other instances of seriation in academic tasks (Kellman and Nyberg, 1980) include:

Science
Ordering by attributes of items within classes
Construction of histograms

Social studies
Showing population densities and typographical maps

Mathematics
Counting (if a student cannot order, then it may be impossible for him or her to count with understanding or refer to the position of an object within a set or the number of objects in a set

Language arts
Ordering of events (chronological order in stories)
Ordering letters of the alphabet for dictionary skills and locating books in the library

Space

Knowledge of space or the world around a person develops in two ways; first, through what Piaget calls perceptual space (what we perceive or what our senses tell us) and second, through representational space (what the mind reconstructs) (Copeland, 1974a).

There are three kinds of spatial relationships:

1. *Topology* includes relations of proximity (nearness, separation, order sequence) and enclosure (surrounding and continuity). Topology is concerned with an object as a thing in isolation, not as it is related to other objects in space. Changes in shape cannot be coordinated with changes in position. At this point, space lacks organization.

2. *Projective* space marks the beginning of attempts to locate objects in relation to one another in order to organize space. It involves the development of perspective or the ability to view an object from different points of view.

3. *Euclidean* Geometric space is concerned with the relation or coordination of objects in space. At this point, the child is able to distinguish and coordinate different viewpoints.

Development

There are three stages of spatial development:

Stage 1 (Sensorimotor and Early Preoperational Period) Topological space is the earliest relationship to develop and deals with surrounds, proximity, and order. It consists of the most general and nonmetric properties of space.

Stage 2 (Late Preoperational Period) Projective space develops and deals with spatial relationships on the horizontal and vertical planes. These relationships are first developed in relation to the body image. Concepts related to the self and objects develop in the following order (Kuczaj and Maratsos, 1975):

1. The child knows the front and back of his or her own body but cannot generalize this information.

2. The child knows the fronts and backs of various objects with fronts, such as cars, telephones and animals.

3. The child can place something in front of or in back of an object with a front and a back.

4. The child knows the sides of his own body and the sides of fronted objects (not left and right but *sides*).

5. The child can generalize his notions of front, back, and side to new objects that he or she has not seen before.

6. The child can use himself or herself as a reference and place something in front, in back, and at the side of nonfronted objects, such as a glass.

Euclidean geometric space appears almost simultaneously with projective space. It involves figures such as line segments, triangles, squares, and circles.

Stage 3 (Concrete Operational Period) Space for the child becomes a coordinate and objective whole when he is around 9 years of age (Copeland, 1974a).

Concept Words (Vocabulary)

The order of the acquisition of vocabulary expressing spatial terms reflects the movement from topological to projective and Euclidean geometric spatial notions. This vocabulary is constrained by the child's cognitive level.

Topological	Projective	Euclidean geometric
at	*over*	*across*
in	*under*	*through*
out	*above*	*along*
on	*below*	*toward*
off	*in front of*	*between*
inside	*in back of*	
outside	*behind*	
top	*beside*	
bottom	*next to*	
	right and *left* (of self 5–8 years)	
	right and *left* (of person he is facing 8–11 years)	

Implications for Instruction

From the time the student enters school, he or she is expected to respond to explanations, directions, and questions containing spatial words. The teacher should be aware of the type of performance that can be expected of the student at each age. Students at the preschool level should be given activities reflecting the topological notions whereas kindergarten and first-grade children can begin to make the transition to projective and Euclidean geometric activities. Problems may occur with some children in the first grade when they are asked to respond to the direction of printing their name at the *top* of the page. This direction requires that the student see the top as a horizontal view, whereas they may have been taught the concepts of *top* and *bottom* from the vertical view (*top* of table, *top* of head, etc.). Prepositional concept words such as *before, after, in front of,* and *next to* require the student to have a concept of the self and its body parts. Otherwise, he or she may experience difficulty in responding to an instruction such as, "Give the book to the child in front of you," or "Put your hands down by your sides."

Other problems in instructional tasks may occur with:

Alphabetizing—requires knowledge of *before* and *after*

Number sequences—requires knowledge of *before, after, left, right*

Social studies—requires knowledge of *across, below, beside, above, next to, along* the axis

Geometry—requires knowledge of *through, along, sides, across, between*

A familiar example of geometric forms found in first-grade workbooks requires the student to judge if the following triangles are congruent or similar.

This task requires the ability of the student to be able to reverse the triangle as well as to be able to understand that the shape does not change the size (conserve). Considering that children in the first grade are beginning the transition into projective space, some difficulty in viewing these triangles from different perspectives may occur. It must also be ascertained as to whether the students have developed reversibility and conservation of spatial objects.

The teacher must determine not only whether the student can recognize and name the shape of a square but also whether he or she understands the concept of square as depicted in other contexts such as signs, boxes, bookcases, and rooms. The generalization of a concept takes place gradually over time.

In this context, the following is an example from a third-grade reading task:

> Mason City, Iowa is a small city near the center of our country. Find Mason City on the map.

The explicit vocabulary representing spatial concepts in this example are *small, center,* and *near*. The implicit concepts included in the request to find the city on the map are *top, bottom, left,* and *right*. If the student has difficulty with this task, the following hypotheses can be drawn:

Hypothesis 1 Does the student understand the concept words of *small, near,* and *center*?

Hypothesis 2 Does the student understand and use the spatial concept words implicit in solving the problem? (These may include *top, bottom, left,* and *right*.)

Hypothesis 3 Does the student understand and use the implicit operations of coordinating vertical and horizontal axes to find the city on the map?

If the student does not have the concept(s) to do the task, the teacher must raise questions as to whether the reason may be developmental, language competence, or lack of experience or instruction.

In summary, spatial relations are important in the learning process because the ability to perceive and understand the words with these relations underlies reading comprehension, computation, and problem solving (Alexander and Nyberg, 1977).

Causality

Multiple classification and understanding of relationships most likely underlie the major portion of abstract thinking. Piaget found that children before 8 years of age were unable to fully understand causal relationships because of the underlying conceptual and linguistic development (Schwebel and Raph, 1973). A young child is likely to consider only one cause or event to the exclusion of others. No single cause can explain a historical, physical, or psychological event (Sigel and Hooper, 1968).

A student of 10 or 11 years of age should have acquired the ability to use classes, relations, measurement, and numbers in a concrete fashion. Children 8–11 years of age are beginning to understand the relationship between physical cause and physical effect, for example, "The sky is very cloudy; it will probably rain."

Sigel and Hooper (1968) discussed three types of causality: (1) physical; (2) social; and (3) psychological and multiplicative. The concept of causality requires the development of the concepts previously discussed. For example, a student 10 years of age generally has acquired a grasp of conservation. He or she can understand that although there may be changes in the physical world, certain things remain constant; likewise, within changes of government, certain institutions remain the same. The student must have acquired the ability of multiple classification to be able to handle the abstractions required to comprehend notions of conflicting ideas and events.

Development

There are four stages in the development of causality:

Stage 1 (Early Preoperational Period) The child attributes to himself or herself or others as being the cause of a given event. Explanations are very subjective.

Stage 2 (Late Preoperational Period) The child 3 years of age and older is trying to find out why things happen. He or she seeks causes and may assume co-occurring events have a causal relationship. This leads to transductive reasoning, e.g., "I had mean thoughts about my brother. He got sick so I made him sick."

Stage 3 (Concrete Operational Period) The understanding of causality that the child develops during this period requires that he or she move from egocentrism and realize that he or she is not the causal agent. The child must have reversibility so that he or she knows what is cause and what is effect. The child must be able to coordinate a series of events.

Stage 4 (Formal Operational Period) The student comprehends all forms of causality because he or she can handle two or more propositions simultaneously.

Concept Words (Vocabulary)

The vocabulary used to express causality includes the words *because, if/then, when, therefore,* and *why*. Some of these words may be used in the late preoperational period, but they do not always reflect causal relationships. They are merely used as conjunctions. The meaningful use denoting causal relationships does not appear until higher levels of cognitive development occur.

Implications for Instruction

Students are presented with material dealing with physical, affective, and social causality, beginning at the early elementary level. For example, second-grade students are requested to give reasons for the causes of night and day when in fact they do not acquire this concept of physical causation until the formal operations period.

Many kindergarten and first grade textbooks contain *if/then* constructions in directions. "If

the ice cubes melt, then what will happen?" The student usually does not have the conceptual skills for this direction until about 8 years of age.

Although students use the *why* question as early as 3 years of age, they do not comprehend *why* questions that imply cause-and-effect relationships and reasoning until about 7 or 8 years of age.

Because history and political science seek causative explanations of events, it is important that the teacher ascertain the student's readiness to do the task in order to prevent task failures.

Critical Thinking

What the student learns is not as important as *how* he learns and communicates the result.

Critical thinking involves evaluation of information . . . it is also creative because it requires the thinker to assimilate information and hypothesize solutions to problems (Feldhusen and Treffinger, 1977, p. 19).

Feldhusen and Treffinger provided five basic steps in critical thinking:

1. Recognizing problems
2. Formulating hypotheses
3. Gathering pertinent facts
4. Testing and evaluation
5. Drawing conclusions

This process is analogous to the development of the process for assessment, discussed in Chapter two. The authors' focus is on helping the teacher develop critical thinking skills in the area of the assessment of language interaction. Feldhusen and Treffinger's focus is to develop critical thinking on the part of the student. Critical thinking is a summary of this chapter. For example:

Critical Thinking Skills
Recognizing problems in observation and recognition
Hypothesizing
Gathering pertinent facts, classifying, comparing relationships
Testing and evaluation; and interpreting
Drawing conclusions; and summarizing

Concept/Operational Skills
Naming/describing attributes
Questioning form and type

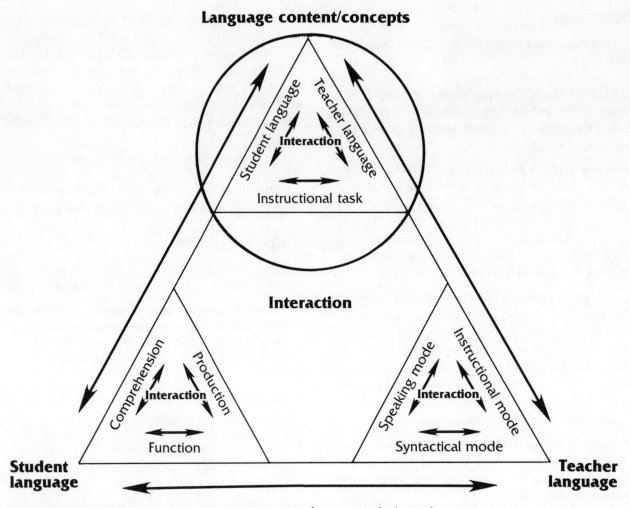

Language content/concepts

Student language
Teacher language
Interaction
Instructional task

Interaction

Comprehension
Production
Interaction
Function

Speaking mode
Instructional mode
Interaction
Syntactical mode

Student language

Teacher language

Figure 4.1 Language content/concepts in the expanded triad.

Simple and multiple grouping, inclusion, exclusion; ordering, conservation, part/whole
Inference; causality; and seriation
Multiple grouping; and conservation

The concept triad consists of three interacting components—content/concepts in the task, concepts in teacher language, and concepts in student language. As indicated in Figure 4.1, most of this chapter is devoted to the content/concepts in the task. For the teacher to become a critical thinker and problem solver of students' learning difficulties in the academics, he or she must be cognizant of the concepts present in the task and the students' level of cognitive development as well as the language (concept words/vocabulary) level that the teacher is using.

Examples of problem-solving tasks inherent in critical thinking are:

1. Transforming or altering an original pattern.
   a. Changing the order of a pattern
   b. Filling in missing parts of the pattern

2. Deriving a solution from a number of clues
   a. Mystery "who done it" problems
   b. Constraint guessing—identifying clues used to derive the solution

3. Choosing a course of action or strategy to solve a problem

   a. What would you do if _____?
   b. How would you _____?

4. Drawing inferences from given facts
   a. What might happen?
   b. Why didn't he _____?
   c. What are the possible alternatives?
   d. Deriving a moral
   e. Changing an ending to a story
   f. Applying a rule to solve a problem
   g. Identifying motives of characters

Summary

Language content/concepts in a task comprise the first component of the basic triad (see Figure 4.1). It is examined in detail in order to provide the teacher with a broader understanding of the complexities of the effect of concepts in learning. In addition to information about the concepts and operations the student must have to perform the instructional task, the teacher must gather information about student language and teacher language before hypotheses about the reasons for student failure can be made.

Procedures for Recording Language Content/Concepts

The specific recording form in Figure 4.2 is designed to help the reader gain experience and practice in analyzing the language content/concepts in an instructional task. By using this form, the information collected can be incorporated in the summary analysis of language interaction so that hypotheses concerning the effects of the interacting components on the students' learning can be formed.

```
I. Explicit—vocabulary
   List vocabulary in:
   A. Instructional task
      _____
      _____
      _____
      _____
      _____

   B. Student response
      _____
      _____
      _____
      _____
      _____

II. Implicit—concept/operations
    Check appropriate line for concept/operations
    in the instructional task.
    _____ Classification
    _____ Conservation
    _____ Time
    _____ Seriation
    _____ Space
    _____ Causality
```

Figure 4.2 Recording form for language content/concepts.

The recording form may be used in two ways:

1. To examine curricular materials and record what implicit and explicit concepts and operations are present in the task

2. To examine and record the implicit and explicit concepts and operations present in a teacher/student interaction

Vocabulary words serve as a cue to determine the implicit concepts/operations present in a particular task.

Review Exercises

This review is designed to help the reader apply the principles discussed in this chapter to actual instructional tasks.

Write the correct *main* concept in the blank space in each of the given examples.

Concepts

Time
Space
Causality
Conservation
Seriation
Classification

Examples

1. a. What number comes after 6?
   b. What comes between?
   c. What number comes between two other numbers in the sequence?
      One answer only: _____

2. a. How are the ducks grouped in this pond?
   b. How are the ducks grouped in the other pond?
   c. What does 6 + 3 equal? What does 4 + 5 equal?
   d. Does 6 + 3 equal 4 + 5?
   e. Are there the same number of ducks in each pond?
      One answer only: _____

3. a. What happened after the hippopotamus cut the rope on the basket?
      One answer only: _____

Write the correct concept or concepts in each of the following examples.

Examples

Concept(s)

1. We can use these braces to frame our picture instead of using our hands. These are called braces. This is a set of _____.

2. Interaction between teacher and student :
Teacher: Mike, I would like you to talk a little bit about your family. Who is the youngest in the family?
Mike: Me and Linda and Laurie.
Teacher: Who is the smallest in the family?
Mike: Laurie.
Teacher: Laurie's the youngest. Do you know how old she is?
Mike: About . . . yeah . . . she's 12.
Teacher: How old are you?
Mike: 13.
Teacher: Now which one is youngest—you or Laurie?
Mike: Me.

3. How many ones in both sets? Make a bundle of 10. How many are left over?

4. At the beginning of the story, what were the three things the little boy liked to eat?

The following examples are from a unit on transportation and deal with various levels of classification. Select the type of classification and indicate the cognitive level.

Type of classification
   Perceptual
   Functional
   Superordinate/categorical

Cognitive level
   Early preoperational
   Late preoperational
   Concrete preoperational
   Formal preoperational

Examples

1. We can put these together because they can all take us places. _____ _____

2. This one has wheels. Give me another one that has wheels. _____ _____

3. How would your own day be different if we didn't have any motor vehicles? _____ _____

4. A horse is an animal, but I am putting him with the vehicles because you can ride on him. _____ _____

5. Tires are made out of rubber and when the truck goes over glass, maybe there will be a blowout. _____ _____

As a further review exercise, the reader may want to evaluate a teaching unit to determine the language content/concept demands involved in the unit. Areas to be evaluated would include: (1) oral and written materials; (2) audiovisual material; (3) required activities; and (4) test questions.

Following are cognitive checklists for the concepts discussed in this chapter.

Classification checklist

Name: _____

Date: _____

Early preoperational	Inability to classify	2–4	*Graphic collections* The student arranges objects randomly. This indicates no system or rational plan although the final arrangement may be a design or represent something such as a face or train.
Late preoperational abilities	Preclassifying	4–6	*Resemblance sorting* The student can group two objects together on the basis of *one* common attribute such as color, shape or size. (matching)
Concrete operational abilities	True classifying	5–7/8	*Logical (additive) classification* The student can group all the objects in a set on the basis of one common attribute (size, shape, color). By age 6–9, he is able to sort by all three criteria.
		6–9	*Relations of "similar" and "belonging to" in classification* The student proceeds from grouping based on a belonging-to relationship to grouping based on similarities, progressing from perceptual to functional to categorical rationales.
		7–8	*Multiplicative classification (matrices)* The student is able to recognize that each item can belong to two or more classes. This involves a more complex logical structure than additive classification. Problems may often be solved fairly early (age 5–7) on a perceptual or graphic level because of the perceptual cues in the matrix.
		8–10	*Multiple class membership* The student can classify an object into more than one category at the same time.
		9–12	*Class inclusion* The students can include one class of objects within a superordinate class.
		10–11	*The null class* The student understands dichotomy of classes and deals with the more abstract notion of a class with something in it and a class with nothing in it (null class).
Formal operational abilities	Flexibility in classifying	12–14	*Horizontal reclassification* The student can classify and then reclassify objects in different ways, realizing that each way is possible at the same time.
		14–15	*Hierarchical reclassification* The student can classify and reclassify hierarchies of increasingly more inclusive classes.

The cognitive checklists were originally developed by a task force of speech and language clinicians in the Madison Metropolitan School District as an assessment tool. Kellman et al. (1982) have rewritten, edited, and modified the original checklist to more completely and accurately reflect Piaget's research. Sources for these checklists include Charles, 1974; Copeland, 1974; Gruber and Vonecke, 1977; Labinowicz, 1980; Laurendeau and Pinard, 1970; Lowery, 1974; and Siegler and Richards, 1979.

Conservation checklist

Name: _____

Date: _____

Early preoperational Inability to establish one-to-one correspondence	2–4	The student is unable to establish one-to-one correspondence; S/he may line up two rows of objects so that the rows are the same length without the same number of objects in each row.
Late preoperational Established one-to-one correspondence; student tends to center on some perceptual attribute rather than using a mental operation to make a judgment.	4–6	One-to-one correspondence with complementary and similar sized sets (dolls/dresses, cups/saucers) with enough items that it requires the child to use a mental operation; objects are arranged in rows. One-to-one correspondence with unlike objects of the same size arranged in rows.
	6–7	*Conservation of number* The objects are arranged in rows as well as in a spatial array that is determined by the examiner; the student understands that quantity of the objects does not change if the physical arrangement of the objects changes.
Concrete operational Students are using logical thinking when making judgments and do not rely on perceptual characteristics.	7–8	*Conservation of length* The length of an object or line remains the same no matter how it is displaced in space. The ability to conserve length is a precursor to work with measurement.
	8–9	*Conservation of solid amount* The amount of a solid (clay) remains the same no matter how its shape is altered or divided. The ability to conserve solid amount is a precursor to work with fractions.
	8–9	*Conservation of liquid amount* The amount (volume) of a liquid remains the same no matter how its shape is altered or divided.
	9–10	*Conservation of discontinuous length* The length of an object or a line remains the same no matter how it is divided (e.g., the sum of the divided parts of a string is equal to its original length.
	9–10	*Conservation of area* The total amount of surface covered by plane geometric shapes remains the same no matter how the shapes are rearranged.
	10–12	*Conservation of weight* The weight of a substance remains the same no matter how its shape is altered or divided.
Formal operational True conservation abilities (Lowery, 1974)	12–14	*Conservation of solid volume* The amount of space occupied by a solid material (blocks) remains the same no matter how its shape is rearranged or transformed.
	14–15	*Conservation of displaced volume* The amount of liquid that object displaces remains the same no matter how the object's shape is changed.

The cognitive checklists were originally developed by a task force of speech and language clinicians in the Madison Metropolitan School District as an assessment tool. Kellman et al. (1982) have rewritten, edited, and modified the original checklist to more completely and accurately reflect Piaget's research. Sources for these checklists include Charles, 1974; Copeland, 1974; Gruber and Vonecke, 1977; Labinowicz, 1980; Laurendeau and Pinard, 1970; Lowery, 1974; and Siegler and Richards, 1979.

Time checklist

Name: _____

Date: _____

Physical time

Sensorimotor Primitive concepts of time develop in this period out of action schemes

0–2½ *Duration* is experienced as waiting time when a child wants to be fed.
Succession is experienced as means and end—as the order of trying to reach an object and then reaching it.

Late sensorimotor to early preoperational (Piagetian Stage I: intuitive time) The student is closely tied to here and now.

1½–4 *Succession* The student is aware of the order of common events and routines.

Late preoperations (Piagetian Stage II: articulated intuitions of time When determining if a student is ready to learn about time, consider that succession is, in a sense, seriation of time and duration is the classification of intervals of time. Coordination of both of these is required for the student to have concepts of operational time. In addition, vocabulary and symbolic representation (numbers on a measuring instrument) of time are involved. Decisions regarding when to initiate instruction and what form it should take to make sense to the student should be based on what is known of his level of funtioning in the areas of seriation, classification, vocabulary, and symbolic representation.

4–6 *Time, speed, and distance* are not differentiated, and the student defines them in terms of the spatial location of stopping points of objects (i.e., anything that has gone faster). Speed concepts are better developed than time concepts in that the student is aware that if one car overtakes another, it is going faster. The student is using his understanding of temporal order (succession) to solve this.

5–6 Relativity of *time labels* are beginning to be understood. The student knows *today* will become *tomorrow* and *tomorrow* will become *today*.

5–7 *Duration* concepts are perceptually bound. The student correctly understands that if you run home faster, it will take less time. Thus, he has an intuitive idea that time and speed are inversely proportional. But s/he incorrectly believes that if a time interval is held constant, and a repetitive task is done in slow motion (like putting marbles in a jar), it will take longer than if it is done with rapid motions. In other words, the student equates more and less work completed with longer and shorter durations.
Succession concepts are stable enough that the student can interpret sentences with an "order of mention" strategy.

Concrete operational (Piagetian Stage III: operational time) The student understands time and can fit the motions of different speeds into a single time/space framework.

6–8 *Succession* or order concepts become stable. The student is able to reverse time order and consider events *before* and *after*. S/he can interpret sentences that have reverse order of mention.

7–8 *Duration* concepts stabilize, and the student can tell which is longer or shorter.

Late concrete operational

9–10 *Recurrence* is coordinated with *succession*; cyclical time concepts develop. The student understands that order of the days of the weeks, months, and seasons repeat themselves. At 8–9 years, the student can associate correct labels with longer and shorter durations. S/he knows a day is shorter than a week.

9–10 *Coordination of succession and duration* The student has operational understanding of succession and duration involving two motions and can synchronize the times of two different motions (e.g., the hour and minute hands on a clock).

Name: _____

Date: _____

9–11	*Transitivity of duration* is understood. It it takes the same time to do *A* and *B*, and the same time to do *B* and *C*, then *A* and *C* can be compared.
9–11	*Transitivity of succession* is understood. If you know the order of events *A* and *B*, and the order of *B* and *C*, the order of *A* and *C* can be compared.
9–11	*Transitivity concepts* are applied to understanding the use of clocks and stop watches to *measure* events occurring at different times.
9–11	*Conservation of time* The student knows that time measured by a clock and a sandglass, or two different clocks, is the same.
9–10	*Class inclusion* is coordinated with duration. The student has the concept that a shorter interval, i.e., a minute is a subset of a longer interval, i.e., an hour.
9–10	*Simultaneity* The student understands that two things can happen at the same time, even if the motions or speeds are different.

Formal operational The student is able to coordinate the concepts and labels of time to approach adult understanding of time. There are some time concepts that continue to remain too difficult for many adults to fully comprehend.

11 +	*Speed and distance concepts* are well-developed but continue to be confused as to how they relate to time. The student does not fully understand the separate concepts of speed, distance, and time until adulthood (Siegler and Richards, 1979).
10–12	The student understands the order of events in historical time A.D.
12–14	The student understands the concepts of A.D. and B.C. and reversed dating in B.C. S/he can understand the order of events in A.D. and B.C.
12–14	The student understands *time zones* around the world.
12–14	The student comprehends the relative aspects of clock time that allow for the creation of daylight savings time.
12–14	The student understands geological time.
14–16	The student understands the concept of light years.

Second stage of formal operational (Copeland, 1974a)

The student is able to understand Einstein's Theory of Relativity.

Time (in terms of age)

Preoperational The student has primitive intuitions of time in terms of age. S/he has an egocentric view of age/time relationships

4–6	The student is unable to coordinate the two ideas of growing and increasing in age. Thus, he believes that age is based on size: whoever is bigger is older.
4–6	The student may think he is older than his parents because he was here when he first saw them.
4–6	S/he believes aging stops when a person is full-grown. Thus, his mother and grandmother are the same age.

Time checklist—*continued*

Name: _____

Date: _____

Early concrete operational Perceptual intuitions of time in terms of age are present	6–8	*The student can use concept of temporal succession to understand that a person born earlier is older and a person born later is younger. The concept of duration helps the student understand that if a person is older than s/he, s/he will always be older. S/he may believe that the amount of experience or knowledge an older person has is proof that the person is older. The student may judge a person as older because of gray hair and wrinkles or other aspects of physical appearance. The student doesn't differentiate ages between becoming fully grown and old age.*
Late concrete operational The student can now use logic to explain age differences. S/he has operational concepts of time in terms of age.	8–10	*Succession* concepts are operational and the student can consider *older than* and *younger than* simultaneously in order to solve problems of *transitivity of age* if the order is explicitly stated.
	8–10	*Duration* concepts are operational and the student can understand *conservation* of age, i.e., the difference in age (in years, months, days) will remain the same no matter how old the person becomes.

The cognitive checklists were originally developed by a task force of speech and language clinicians in the Madison Metropolitan School District as an assessment tool. Kellman et al. (1982) have rewritten, edited, and modified the original checklist to more completely and accurately reflect Piaget's research. Sources for these checklists include Charles, 1974; Copeland, 1974; Gruber and Vonecke, 1977; Labinowicz, 1980; Laurendeau and Pinard, 1970; Lowery, 1974; and Siegler and Richards, 1979.

Seriation checklist

Name: _____

Date: _____

Early preoperational True seriation is not occurring; The student compares objects in a global sense using polar opposites.

2–3   The student is able to compare two objects when differences are obvious in terms of polar opposites.

3–4   When presented with a group of seven or more objects, the student will place items in arrays of two or three, using a trial-and-error strategy. S/he cannot combine the arrays.

3–4   The student is beginning to develop comprehension of opposities and comparative language forms.

Late preoperational The student utilizes concept of one-to-one correspondence in seriating ten items; s/he can use different materials. A trial-and-error strategy is still utilized.

4–5   The student can construct a series of four to seven objects using trial and error; s/he can insert additional elements by further trial-and-error and usually starts the task over to add an additional item.

4–5   The student can construct a series of objects by length but often pays attention to only one end of each object.

Transitional The student is less dependent on perceptual judgments. S/he may still revert to a trial-and-error strategy.

$5\frac{1}{2}$–7   The student can arrange both dolls and sticks in order and make the serial correspondence of the right stick to the right doll, largely by trial-and-error.

6–7   The student can construct a "stairway" of 7–10 cuisenaire rods or blocks by length paying attention to both ends. *note:* seriation of weight develops approximately 2 years later than seriation by size and length.

6–7   The student can insert additional elements in the proper place in the series, but frequently reverts to a trial-and-error strategy.

Concrete operational The student has a strategy for solving the seriation problem that does not depend on trial and error (measurement). The procedure is organized and exhaustive; the student demonstrates transitivity and reversibility. However, objects must still be available.

7–8   The student uses a systematic strategy to scan and seriate ten items by size from largest to smallest.

7–8   The student uses comparative and superlative forms of adjectives to describe comparisons between objects.

The student can reverse the procedure to seriate ten items from smallest to largest.

The student recognizes that any given element is both larger than the preceding and smaller than those that follow it ($E > D$, C, and $D < F$, G), the transitive asymmetrical relation.

7–8   The student can insert three items in an array of seven without resorting to trial-and-error. S/he can use ordinal number as a strategy when solving insertion of one element in a double-seriation task.

$6\frac{1}{2}$–8   The student can complete a double seriation, i.e., find the biggest girl and the biggest umbrella, then look for the next biggest girl and umbrella, etc.

9–10   The student can use the idea of ordinal number in a double seriation task so that when one series (the girls, for example) is spread out, the student can still tell which umbrella goes with which girl by counting from one end of the row.

Name: _____

Date: _____

(Piaget makes a distinction between multiple seriation and multiple classification, but found children able to perform both at approximately the same time.)

7–8   Given a set of nuts and bolts, or jars and lids, the student can immediately put together the two with corresponding size. Trial-and-error strategies are not apparent.

7–9   Given a set of objects which may be arranged in order according to two variables, such as leaves graded by size and color, the student immediately recognizes the two variables, begins to order the leaves by one or the other variable, and works consistently toward a solution which accommodates both variables. The end result is a matrix.

9–10   When the examiner shuffles double-seriated objects and randomly pulls out one item, the student can find corresponding item in another series.

9–10   When verbal-ordering problems involving transitivity are presented to students capable of solving similar problems with physical materials, they may experience difficulty even though the problem is written down. Nine- to ten-year-olds who are able to solve verbal transitivity problems appear to be using a strategy other than propositional logic, i.e., past experience, visual imagery, etc. to solve the problem.

Formal operational   The student at this stage is able to represent how an ordered group will look prior to ordering the objects physically; Thus, s/he is able to draw conclusions not only through direct observation, but also from hypothetical statements; At this stage, the student is able to consider an infinite series. S/he can ignore the content and focus on the form of the relations.

11–12+   The student draws a representation of ten items in order before s/he orders them.

11–12+   The student can solve verbally stated problems requiring the understanding of transitivity.

  The student uses logical thinking strategies to solve problems when the physical materials are not visible. Information is presented abstractly through hypotheses having the form *if/then*.

11–12+   The student can seriate abstract and hypothetical arrays. For example, rank a list of historical figures in order of their importance, use rating scale of numbers from one to five, complete opinion polls indicating support for political figures/decisions from *strongly agree* to *strongly disagree*, etc.

The cognitive checklists were originally developed by a task force of speech and language clinicians in the Madison Metropolitan School District as an assessment tool. Kellman et al. (1982) have rewritten, edited, and modified the original checklist to more completely and accurately reflect Piaget's research. Sources for these checklists include Charles, 1974; Copeland, 1974; Gruber and Vonecke, 1977; Labinowicz, 1980; Laurendeau and Pinard, 1970; Lowery, 1974; and Siegler and Richards, 1979.

Name: _____
Date: _____

Sensorimotor Concepts of space begin to develop in this period as the infant's random explorations become more refined and purposeful. The coordination of motor activity and vision lays the groundwork for acquisition of further spatial knowledge; Piaget describes children's actions on objects that begin to allow him/her to abstract shapes, understand distance, and mentally represent shapes and their relationships in space.

Birth–2

Early preoperational Between ages 2–4, spatial relations are seen as components of *topological space*. Topological relations include *proximity* (nearness, farness); *separation* (distinguishing one object from another, parts from wholes); *order* (coordination of time and space); and *enclosure* (open/closed figures).

2–4   *Perceptual and representational space* The student views space from a topological perspective. S/he can distinguish between open/closed forms, two holes, dot inside or outside of a closed figure, or intertwined or overlapping forms; student cannot distinguish between circles and squares as Euclidean shapes; both are topologically closed figures.

Late preoperational/transitional (Euclidean and projective space[a]) These concepts develop simultaneously. The student begins to use an operational method of grouping the elements perceived (i.e., angles, number of sides, distance between angles, etc.). Grouping is dependent on beginning at a fixed point on the figure, tracing the outline, and being able to reverse the process. The student mentally groups these sensory impressions into a coordinated whole. S/he can coordinate different perspectives of an object and adjust to variations in size and position.

4–5   The student can view space from a Euclidean perspective; can distinguish a square from a circle and can find another square or rectangle (perceptual task) but cannot necessarily copy it (representational task).

4–6   The student can distinguish shapes with curved sides and those with straight sides. S/he does not distinguish circles from ellipses or squares from rectangles.

4–5   *Order (topological)* The student begins to be able to duplicate a simple bead pattern if s/he can check the model constantly and if the spatial arrangement is not transformed.

4–6   *Reversed order* The student can maintain the mental image of bead order entering and existing from a tube.

The student can predict the order of exit after rotation of the tube.

4–6   The student can make a straight line using a table edge as a guide.

5–6 or 7   The student can differentiate shapes by the number of angles; by age 6, the student is operational for Euclidean shapes. Account is now taken of order and distance between points on a figure.

6–7   The student can represent geometric shapes. Angles and proportions are appropriate.

6–7   *Order*
a. The student can match a linear order.
b. The student can transpose a linear order to a circular order.
c. The student is able to reverse the order.

Name: _____

Date: _____

	6–7	The student can make a straight line immediately regardless of where the end points are located using a sighting strategy.
	5–8	*Left/right spatial relations* The student can correctly identify his/her own right and left hands, feet, etc.
	6–7	*Spatial coordinates* The student is unable to draw the water level in a series of tilted jars, s/he indicates a line parallel to the base or side of the jar.
Concrete operational In concrete operations, the student has the ability to transform spatial relationships mentally. S/he can mentally represent or draw on paper relationships that are not visible; S/he has learned and can abstract and represent the properties of Euclidean shapes.	8–9	*Spatial coordinates* The student has developed the necessary horizontal and vertical reference systems which allow him/her to draw the water level in a bottle correctly, regardless of the tilt.
	8–9	*Perspective* The student is able to draw something as it would appear from a different perspective.
	7 or 8	The student can make a series of successively shorter line segments and realize the possibility of a large number of subdivisions. S/he cannot conceptualize the number of subdivisions as being infinite.
	8–11	*Left/right relations* The student is able to understand that the opposition of left and right is relative to the viewpoint of the other person.
	9–12	The student is able to correctly identify the relative position of three nonfronted objects in terms of left and right.
	9–12	*Perspective* The student is able to coordinate perspectives as they are viewed from other positions.
Formal operational	11–12	*Perspective* The student is able to consider the perspective of complex figures such as single and double cones.
	11–12	*Continuity and infinity* The student is able to envision the subdivision of a line into an infinite number of points in space; these points have no shape or surface.
	11–13	*Spatial coordinates* The student can draw to scale using ratio and proportion, s/he has abstracted vertical and horizontal coordinates, s/he no longer needs physical objects as a reference system.

The cognitive checklists were originally developed by a task force of speech and language clinicians in the Madison Metropolitan School District as an assessment tool. Kellman et al. (1982) have rewritten, edited, and modified the original checklist to more completely and accurately reflect Piaget's research. Sources for these checklists include Charles, 1974; Copeland, 1974; Gruber and Vonecke, 1977; Labinowicz, 1980; Laurendeau and Pinard, 1970; Lowery, 1974; and Siegler and Richards, 1979.

[a] Projective properties of a figure are those which are not changed if the figure is projected onto a plane surface, i.e., casting a shadow. Euclidean properties are the actual lengths and measurements.

Causality checklist

Name: _____

Date: _____

Sensorimotor The student's behavior reflects the means/end process of sensory expoloration. The student cannot mentally represent this action.

0–2 The student understands causality only in terms of his own actions. S/he experiments with pulling, thrusting, launching, etc., which leads to "magical-phenomalistic" ideas of causality in pre operations. That is, the occurrence of two events close together in time makes them appear to be causally related. The causal relationship is centered on the student's own action on the object without consideration for the spatial relationship between cause and effect.

Preoperational Intuitive thoughts The student's view of the world as seen through symbolic play is the only view possible for him/her. S/he questions incessantly to develop a sense of reality. S/he begins to realize that things don't happen by chance and that every effect must have a cause. The student views the world with him/herself as a model. Thus, everything active must be alive. Reasoning is transductive. That is, the student's thinking moves from particular to particular and s/he sees a causal relationship between simultaneous events whether there is one or not.

3–5 The student's responses to causality problems reflect the following kinds of logic:
Motivational responses The student believes that human motivation is the cause of everything. Things don't happen by chance; God or man causes everything (wind, rain, etc.).
Phenomenistic responses The student relates two facts that occur close together in time or space and assigns a causal relationship. The moon doesn't fall down because there is no sun.
Finalistic responses The student states that things are the way they are because they are. The river runs because it runs to the sea.
Magical responses The student believes that one's gestures, thoughts, words, etc. influence people and events. "Step on a crack, you'll break your mother's back."
Moralistic responses The student believes that events occur because they have to; it wouldn't be right if they didn't. The sun sets so we can have night.

Late preoperational/transitional The number of *why* questions begins to diminish. The student becomes less egocentric and starts to consider other's viewpoint.S/he also begins to justify his/her own view point. Circular explanations are still common when the student is asked to explain complex events. Events which are beyond the student's ability to understand still resist logical explanation and the student may revert to transductive reasoning which is more characteristic of preoperational thought.

5–7 or 8 The student's responses to causality problems reflect the following kinds of logic:
Artificial responses The student believes that objects and occurrences are manmade. When asked about the origin of the sun, the student replies that men made it so we can have light. Although students of 7–8 years in age can explain the dissolving of a solid in terms of tiny particles, they are unable to explain changes of state i.e. melting, boiling.
Animistic responses The student believes that non-living things have life and consciousness. By age 7–8, inanimate objects are no longer living; thus students at this age learn to deal with death in realistic terms.

Concrete operational By the end of concrete operations, the student can think in abstract terms and made logical explanations. The student sees causal relationships as reversible.

8–11 The student's responses to causality problems reflect the following kinds of logic:
Mechanical responses This kind of reasoning replaces animistic reasoning. Thus, a bicycle goes because of its pedals, clouds move because of wind.
Generative responses These responses refer to the origins of things rather than their movements. Previously the student believed that things were made by God or man; now s/he believes that objects are made by other objects. Thus the sun comes from a cloud, clouds come from smoke.

Name: _____

Date: _____

Logical responses Logical reasoning begins to emerge around age 10–11. It depends on the student's ability to consider evidence in an open-minded way. It includes both inductive reasoning (inferences or generalizations made from observations of a number of specific occurrences) and deductive reasoning (generalizations based on logic without the need for physical evidence).

Formal operational (Charles, 1974; Gruber and Vonecke, 1977.)   11–12+   Explanations are considerably more comprehensive and theoretical. Formal thinkers able to explain physical phenomena of both distant objects (such as the solar system), and invisible objects (such as molecular and atomic models).

The cognitive checklists were originally developed by a task force of speech and language clinicians in the Madison Metropolitan School District as an assessment tool. Kellman et al. (1982) have rewritten, edited, and modified the original checklist to more completely and accurately reflect Piaget's research. Sources for these checklists include Charles, 1974; Copeland, 1974; Gruber and Vonecke, 1977; Labinowicz, 1980; Laurendeau and Pinard, 1970; Lowery, 1974; and Siegler and Richards, 1979.

References

Alexander, M., and Nyberg, B. 1977. PLANT (Piaget Language Analyze New Territory). Madison Metropolitan School District, Madison, WI.

Bloom, L. (ed.). 1978. Readings in Language Development. John Wiley and Sons, Inc., New York.

Carpenter, T., Corbitt, M., Kepner, Jr., H., Lindquist, M., and Reys, R. 1981. Results from the Second Mathematics Assessment of Educational Progress. The National Council of Teachers of Mathematics, Inc., Reston, VA.

Carroll, J. 1977. Developmental parameters of reading comprehension. In: J. Guthrie (ed.), Cognition, Curriculum, and Comprehension. International Reading Assn., Newark, DE.

Charles, C. M. 1974. Teacher's Petit Piaget. Fearon Pubs., Inc., Belmont, CA.

Copeland, R. W. 1974a. Diagnostic and Learning Activities in Mathematics for Children. Macmillan, New York.

Copeland, R. W. 1974b. How Children Learn Mathematics. Macmillan, New York.

Elkind, D., and Flavell, J. (eds.). 1969. Studies in Cognitive Development Essays in Honor of John Piaget. Oxford University Press, New York.

Feldhusen, J. F., and Treffinger, D. J. 1977. Teaching Creative Thinking and Problem Solving. Kendall/Hunt Publishing Co., Dubuque, IA.

Gruber, H. E., and Voneche, J. J. 1977. The Essential Piaget. Basic Books, Inc., New York.

Gruenewald, L. J. 1972. Teaching classification skills to handicapped children. Unpublished doctoral dissertation, University of Wisconsin, Madison.

Inhelder, G., and Piaget, J. 1964. The Early Growth of Logic in the Child—Classification and Seriation. Routledge and Keegan Paul Ltd., London.

Kamii, C., and Peper, R. 1969. A Piagetian Method of Evaluating Preschool Children's Development in Classification. Ypsilanti Michigan Public Schools July.

Kean, J. M., and Personke, C. 1976. The Language Arts, Teaching and Learning in the Elementary School. St. Martins Press, New York.

Kellman, M., Lyngaas, K., and Nyberg, B. 1982. Cognitive Checklist. Madison Metropolitan School District, Madison, WI.

Kellman, M. and Nyberg, B. 1980. Piaget and the Curriculum, An In-service Course for Teachers. Madison Metropolitan School District, Madison, WI.

Kuczaj, S., and Maratsos, M. 1975. On the acqui- sition of front, back, and side. Child Develop. 46:202–210, March.

Labinowicz, X. (ed.). 1980. The Piaget Primer. Addison-Wesley Publishing Co., Menlo Park, CA.

Laurendeau, M., and Pinard, A. 1970. The Development of the Concept of Space in the Child. International Universities Press, Inc., New York.

Lowery, L. 1974. Learning about Learning Series. University of California, Berkeley, CA.

McGuire, M., and Bumpus, N. 1971. Reading Comprehension Skills. Croft Educational Services, New London, CT.

Piaget, J., and Inhelder, B. 1969. The Psychology of the Child. Basic Books, Inc., New York.

Pulaski, M. 1971. Understanding Piaget. Harper and Row Publishers, Inc., New York.

Rice, M. 1980. Cognition to Language Categories, Word Meanings, and Training. University Park Press, Baltimore.

Schwebel, M., and Raph, J. (eds.). 1973. Piaget in the Classroom. Basic Books, Inc., New York.

Sigel, I., and Hooper, F. (eds.). 1968. Logical Thinking in Children. Holt, Rinehart and Winston, Inc., New York.

Siegler, R. S., and Richards, D. D. 1979. Development of time, speed, and distance concepts. Develop. Psychol. 15:288–298.

Smith, B. O. 1983. Curriculum content. In: F. W. English (ed.), Fundamental Curriculum Decisions. Assn. for Supervision and Curriculum Development, DC.

Voyat, G. 1973. The development of operations: A theoretical and practical matter. In: M. Schwebel and J. Raph (eds.), Piaget in the Classroom. Basic Books, Inc., New York.

Suggested Readings

Carroll, J. 1964. Language and Thought. Prentice-Hall, Inc., Englewood Cliffs, N.J.
This book provides an overview concerning the relationship between language and cognition. The theme of this book is that thought and cognition are presupposed by language and that speech is a consequence of some kind of thought and cognition, even though language structure may influence thought.

Engelmann, S. 1969. Conceptual Learning. Dimensions in Early Learning Series, Dimensions Publishing Co., CA.
Englemann's approach provides a very specific methodology in analyzing concepts, tasks and the

development of teaching strategies for teaching the concepts within a group situation in the classroom.

Fennema, E. (ed.) 1981. Mathematics Education Research: Implications for the '80s. National Council of Teachers of Mathematics, Reston, VA.

Flavell, J. H. 1982. On cognitive development. Child Develop. 3:1–10. February.

Gorman, R. 1972. Discovering Piaget, A Guide for Teachers. Charles E. Merrill Publishing Co., Columbus, OH.
This is a self-instructional book for teachers. It provides an overview of Piaget's stages and uses that information to raise issues concerning curriculum development in preschool through secondary programming.

Guthrie, J., (ed.)1977. Cognition, Curriculum, and Comprehension. International Reading Assn., Newark, DE.
This book of readings provides a tremendous amount of information concerning the importance of analyzing linguistic and cognitive factors inherent in curriculum as applied to the task of learning to read.

Hallahan, D. P. (ed.) 1980. Teaching Exceptional children to use cognitive strategies. Except. Educ. Q. 1.

Lavatelli, C. S. 1970a. Piaget's Theory Applied to An Early Childhood Curriculum. A Center for Media Development Incorporated Book. American Science Engineering Inc., Boston.

Lavatelli, C. S. 1970b. Teacher's Guide for Early Childhood Curriculum—A Piaget Program. A Center for Media Development Incorporated Program. American Science Engineering Inc., Boston.

Laycock, M., and Watson, G. 1971. The Fabric of Mathematics, A Resource Book for Teachers. Activities Resource Co., Hayward, CA.

Raths, L., Jonas, A. Rothstein, A. and Wassermann, S. 1967. Teaching for Thinking, Theory and Application, Charles E. Merrill Publishing Co., Columbus, OH.

Weikart, D., Rogers, L., Adcock, C., and McClelland, D. 1971. The Cognitively Oriented Curriculum. High/Scope Educational Research Foundation, Ypsilanti, MI. (Publications Dept., National Assn. for the Education of Young Children, 1834 Connecticut Ave., N.W., Washington, D.C.)

Williams, E., and Shuard, H. 1970. Primary Mathematics Today. Longman Group Ltd., London.

Chapter 5
Teacher Language

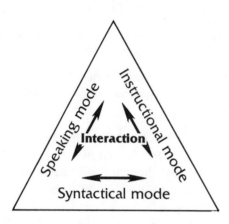

Instructional mode
Speaking mode
Interaction
Syntactical mode

The language used by the teacher in an instructional context directly and indirectly affects the responses of the students. This chapter assesses the instructional language (the oral language of the teacher as well as the written language of the curriculum) in order to determine the extent to which it is a contributing factor in the student's failure in academic tasks.

GOALS

1. To provide the reader with information about each component of instructional language.
2. To analyze information on each component of instructional language.

3. To provide a strategy for recording information on each component of instructional language.
4. To provide information on the use of questions in instruction.

The language used by the classroom teacher directly and indirectly influences the responses of the students, as shown in the following exchange between a teacher and students, 6 years of age, in a Title I language experience class.

Sequencing task

To put together four cards depicting children building a snowman (Sequencing implies the ability to perceive the gestalt of the task rather than rely on specific perceptual clues.)

Teacher: Annie and Joel, today we are going to play a game and we are going to give you some cards. They are a mixed-up story. The things that happened aren't in order. What I would like you to do is to look at each of the pictures and

put the things together the way they would happen in the story. Let's take all your cards and put them out so you can see them. Please start.
Joel: What do we have to do?
Teacher: Now, let's look at the pictures and decide which things happened first in the story. Good. Now let's find what might have happened next.

(Joel finished putting the cards in order.)

Teacher: Now, Joel, can you tell me the story of what happened?
Joel: Of what?
Teacher: Of what happened in these pictures. Tell me the story. What happened?
Joel: Beats me.
Teacher: What happened first?
Joel: There was nothing.

Teacher: There was nothing? Weren't there any children in the first picture? What was there?

Joel: Just a pile of snow.

Teacher: Just a pile of snow. Good Joel! What happened next?

Joel: The kids made only one snowball.

Teacher: Good. They made one snowball—the bottom one. Then what happened?

Joel: Then they put two more balls on.

In this exchange, it is apparent that the student's responses were directly related to the teacher's use of language in giving directions and asking questions. It is not even certain whether the student understood the actual expectations of the teacher. Barnes (1971) stated that:

Pupils are left to guess what is wanted more by attention to the teacher's hints than by understanding of the matter in hand (p. 240).

Before the teacher can determine whether the students are able to do the task of sequencing, he or she would have to modify his or her own language to elicit the specific responses required from the students.

The language of curricular materials (workbooks and textbooks) have built-in language and concept difficulties. Teachers often are frustrated because they do not know how to analyze or modify the textbook language.

How would a first-grade student be expected to respond to the following direction (Foresman, 1971, p. 25):

Task	Instructions
Body parts	Put your finger under the next word beside the picture that shows the front of the girl. What do you think the word is? Is there another arm besides the one that is labeled?
Recognition and labeling	

Barnes (1971) stated:

Teacher's view of language in the classroom can be characterized in terms of student's response instead of in terms of learning. In terms of learning, teachers need to take more responsibility for their use of language in instruction and to direct their attention to those aspects of instructional relationships which are *relevant to the student's use of language for learning* (p. 240).

Teacher Language

Research on teacher language behavior reveals the following characteristics (Amidon and Flanders, 1967; Bellack et al., 1966; Berlin, et al., 1980; Pollak and Gruenewald, 1974; Weigand, 1979):

1. Teachers dominate classroom conversation by talking most of the time.

2. Teacher talk consists primarily of explanations, directions, and questions.

3. The type of teacher questions are usually narrow (requiring one- to three-word responses).

Indirect influence refers to the types of statements that increase the student's freedom to respond, whereas direct influence includes statements that restrict the student's response.

In summary, when teachers talk within an instructional task, they seem to constrain the interaction in a variety of ways. To analyze the effect, the teacher should become familiar with three modes of teacher language: speaking, instructional, and syntactical (see Figure 5.1).

Speaking Mode
(Length, Rate, and Intonation)

Amidon and Flanders (1967) presented the "law of two-thirds."

According to this law, two-thirds of the time spent in classrooms is devoted to talk, two-thirds of this talking time is occupied by the teacher, and two-thirds of teacher talk consists of direct influence (Dunkin and Biddle, 1974, p. 54).

An excessive *amount* of talking tends to create nonlisteners or at best, passive or confused listeners. The following classroom example is a case in point.

Teacher: The first thing we are going to do—I want to ask you to think whether or not you have to do adding or subtracting first. Think really hard. Just do the whole problem. Don't just write down plus or minus. Just do the whole problem whether you think it is adding or subtracting. Okay, let's see. Would you please put your sign down so I know exactly what you did. Okay, and let's see—David, you said you plussed 36 and 53 and Debbie, you said you

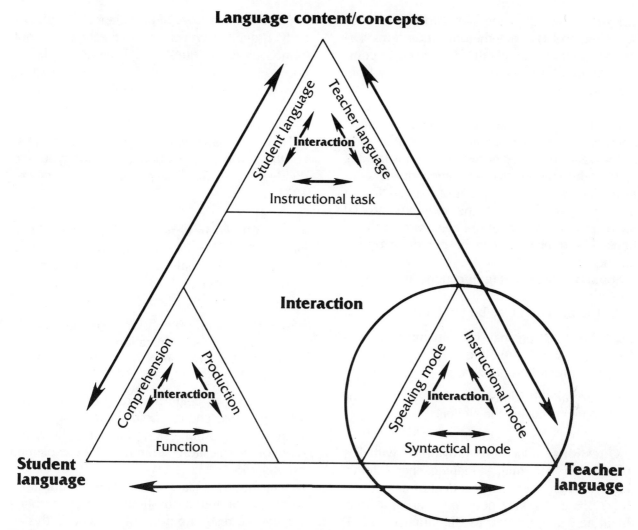

Language content/concepts

Student language   Teacher language

Interaction

Instructional task

Interaction

Comprehension   Production

Interaction

Function

Speaking mode   Instructional mode

Interaction

Syntactical mode

**Student
language**

**Teacher
language**

Figure 5.1 Teacher language in the expanded triad.

plussed also. Okay what were the key words in that story?

The students who were expected to do the story problems in this classroom did not know how or where to begin and on the whole, failed the task. The teacher repeated the direction with examples. The repetition was as long and complicated as in the first instance. Furthermore, the direct teacher influence did not provide opportunities for the student to *use* verbal language and to become an active problem solver and critical thinker. The teacher needs assistance in order to become aware of the *amount* and *length* of what he or she is saying as well as the complex language he or she is using. This insight enables the teacher to determine whether the length of the direction and irrelevant information is restricting the student's response.

The rate of the teacher's speech, whether too fast or too slow, also may interfere with the student's comprehension of what is being said.

Intonation refers to the variations in pitch and stress of speech. In the sentences, "*He* hit him," "He *hit* him," and "He hit *him*," the meaning may vary, depending on the word that is being stressed.

Because many teachers feel that it is their job to give information and the students' job to listen, the effect of the amount, rate, and intonation (speaking mode) on the student is often overlooked.

Instructional Mode
(Explanations/Directions and Questions)

Explanations/Directions *Explanation* in the instructional mode includes: 1) Explaining the task or activity; 2) giving facts and opinions; 3) lecturing; and 4) asking rhetorical questions. *Directions* include: 1) specific directions; 2) commands; and 3) orders requiring a response from the student.

Teachers must be aware that an explanation often accompanies a direction. If the explanation is not well-formulated or the direction is lacking clarity, the student may become equally confused. Recording the amount of explanation or direction given by the teacher may be a crucial factor in analyzing a failure situation. Explanations, like directions, can be overdone by the teacher.

Some pitfalls in giving directions are:

1. The direction may be too long.

2. The direction may contain multiple concepts, which are difficult for the student to remember and process.

3. Several directions may be given at one time, confusing the student.

Questions *Questions* provide us with key information regarding student/teacher interaction. Teachers spend a great deal of time giving directions and asking questions during instructional activities. In fact, as Cunningham (1971) pointed out, teachers often ask too many questions. This may result in little opportunity for students to ask questions. Elementary teachers ask approximately three and one-half to six and one-half questions per minute (Floyd, 1960; Cunningham, 1971). Rowe (1969) stated that teachers expect students to answer questions immediately and then will repeat or rephrase the answer and ask another question in slightly less than a second. Teachers think that a rapid series of questions will gain the student's attention. The fast repetition of questions does not give students time to think or phrase the answer. It only confuses them. Cole and Williams (1973) showed that the type of question (narrow or broad) that the teacher asks directly affects the response of the students. This effect occurs not only in the content of the student's response (level of thinking) but also in its structure (syntax and length).

Unfortunately, the art of asking questions that are both instructional and diagnostic is not an innate skill (Yanicke, 1975). It requires practice if it is to reach a level of proficiency. Despite its daily usage, however, most teachers are not trained in asking questions. They do not know how to ask a *good* question, nor do they know how to utilize questions appropriately (Guszak, 1967; Melnik, 1968; Torrance and Myers, 1973; Sanders, 1966; Rogers, 1972).

There are many ways to chart question types. For the purpose of this book, question types are divided into two categories (Cunningham, 1971).

Question type		Question form
Narrow (N):	Predictable	*what, who,*
	Factual	*where, is,*
	Recall	*which, can,*
		do
Broad (B):	Comprehension	*why, how,*
	Generalization	*what if,*
	Inference	*could it be*

It is easier to begin recording question types with only two choices before analyzing the hierarchy of question-asking behavior. Development of the question hierarchy will be explained on page 55.

Many times, a teacher asks repeated questions to clarify the initial questions in order to obtain the desired response from the student. In this attempt at clarification, the teacher may indeed confuse the student because he or she asked inappropriate questions in the first place (wrong question type) or used the wrong question form. Question type refers to the level of thinking (narrow or broad) demanded from the student. Recalling facts, naming places, identifying, or a *yes* or *no* reply is a lower level of thinking. Forming a generalization, making an inference, or relating cause and effect is a higher level of thinking.

Similarly, the form of the question will affect the student's response. The form refers to the *wh* word being used in the question. However, this may be incorrectly expressed. The word *what* can be used in both narrow and broad questions:
1. *What* are the boys doing? (narrow)
2. *What* if the boys would do that? (broad)
The difference in the question form depends upon the words that follow the *wh* word. In charting, you must listen to the entire question and the response required before recording the type as broad or narrow.

It is very important to note that broad questions are not necessarily better than narrow questions. Their appropriateness depends upon the academic task, the teacher's expectations or objectives for that task, and the language level of the students.

On the other hand, continually asking narrow questions of students will not assist them in using language to develop the higher levels of thinking that are required by academic tasks in upper elementary grades. The teacher should vary his or her questions in order to allow the students sufficient practice in using language to develop levels of thinking required by advanced tasks in math and reading comprehension.

A review of the literature on question asking (Yanicke, 1975) shows that approximately 60% of the questions teachers ask are cognitive memory questions (i.e., narrow questions requiring recall or recognition of known facts); another 20% are procedural questions (i.e., those involved in management, such as "Would you take this to the office?"); and only 20% require the pupil to think (Gall, 1970). There are several reasons why teachers may use memory questions in excess instead of exploring the whole cognitive continuum with their students. Teacher-training programs most often focus on *content* courses (reading, science, social studies, mathematics), often referred to as method courses, and not on *process*. Questions can be classified as process and therefore have not received much attention. Another reason why teachers seem to persist in asking memory questions is that when they use higher cognitive questions, they have experienced an increase in student failures (Carin and Sund, 1971; Hunkins, 1976; Minnis and Schrabel, 1970; and Taba, 1967).

> Since correct answers play an important role in the educational system, teachers quickly return to the memory questions where they get correct answers. Finally, it is quite possible that teachers do not know why they ask questions (Yanicke, 1975, p. 2).

Syntactical Mode

Syntactical mode is defined as word order and sentence complexity. Sentence complexity refers to simple, compound, and complex sentences. A simple sentence is defined as containing a subject, verb, and object; a compound sentence is composed of two or more simple sentences; a complex sentence includes dependent and independent clauses connected by conjunctions.

Many problems incurred in learning a specific instructional task are attributable primarily to the fact that the teacher's use of syntax and vocabulary may make it difficult for the student to understand directions, explanations, and questions. The same problem also is true in some instructional texts. The following syntax and vocabulary may be utilized in a first-grade math lesson constructed by the teacher.

> Now we have put the members of the two sets together. This is the set of the ball and the block. The set of the ball put together with the set of the block is equal to the set of the ball and the block.

If students experience problems with this task, teachers need to hypothesize: (1) whether the syntax is too complex; (2) whether the direction is too long; or (3) whether the vocabulary (*put together, equal, set,* and *members*) is understood.

Teachers question whether modifying their syntactical behavior means "talking down" to a student. On the contrary, it means utilizing language that is relevant and within the student's experience. Even more complex is this example (Suppes and Suppes, 1968):

> The difference of the set whose members are the book, the chalk, and the eraser and the set whose member is the book is the set whose members are the chalk and the eraser (p. 74).

The effect of the three modes of teacher language (speaking, instructional, and grammatical) are demonstrated in the following example, in which a teacher engages her seven learning-disabled students, (chronological age 8–9 years) in a math problem involving missing addends. (Problems pertaining to each segment are noted in parentheses):

Task
$8 + \square = 12$
$\square + 2 = 5$

Teacher: In this activity, we will be using fist and fingers as a manipulative device. In a missing addend equation, the fist represents the known addend. When the results are unknown, the known addends are represented by fingers. Today, boys, we are going to learn how to plus two different kinds of problems. The first type is where they tell you the number that you are supposed to plus. This one says "6 + 7 equals □." Can you think of a story where we have 6 plus 7 equals a number? Can you think of six bunnies or deer?

(*Problems here include long explanation, confusing vocabulary, and complex syntax.*)

Response: Six rabbits.

Teacher: We can have six rabbits plus seven what?

(*This is an unclear question.*)

Response: Seven deer.

Teacher: Of course, six rabbits plus seven deer equals how many animals? Boys, when it doesn't say equals a number then we have fingers. Right? Of course, how many fingers does it tell you to plus in this problem? Let's put it on the board. We have six rabbits plus seven deer equals how many animals?

(*The teacher here presents confusing vocabulary, long directions and questions, and her form of questions is confusing.*)

Teacher: Jimmy, could you tell us the next problem.

Jimmy: 9 + 4 = □.

Teacher: Jimmy, could you tell us why you had to plus fingers? What did you look at that told you you had to plus fingers and fists?

Jimmy: No response.

Obviously, the teacher did not analyze the language in the textbook from which she took this task. There was no way the teacher could determine whether her students understood how to do the missing addends until her own language was modified to use the appropriate and relevant vocabulary, syntax, question, directions, and explanations. Instruction has to be planned—not only how the task should be learned but also what language should be used

to teach it. The next section suggests ways in which the teacher can obtain this objective information.

If the teacher is to intervene in student task failure, it is imperative that he or she engage in the analysis of the instructional language used. This enables the teacher to determine how much of the task failure is attributable to the language or other variables.

Recording Teacher Language

For a teacher to observe and record his or her own language can become a lengthy, complex, and absorbing activity. There are many ways to record teacher language interaction. Most are complex and require substantial training in order to maintain reliability. These procedures sometimes deter teachers from engaging in self-analysis. An informal method of recording may be more acceptable to many teachers and will give essential information. For the brave and hearty souls interested in pursuing a more expanded and reliable view of recording, an adapted version (Pollak and Gruenewald, 1978) of the Amidon and Flanders model (1967) is included in this book (see Appendix).

Teachers also may be understandably reluctant to participate in this activity for several reasons:

1. It may be a time-consuming task.
2. It makes some persons uncomfortable to listen to their voice.
3. It is frustrating and disappointing to hear that what was intended to be conveyed did not occur.

However uncomfortable or difficult it may be, the rewards for the teacher who examines his or her own language are high. Success in teaching is well worth the effort.

Suggested Procedures for Informal Recording

Step 1 (Audiotaping) Tape-record a small segment of a lesson (no longer than 5 minutes) with an individual student who is experiencing difficulty in learning the task. The lesson must be an exchange between student and teacher.

Step 2 (Listening) Listening skills develop over time. Therefore, listen for one item (see below) each time the tape is played back. As listening skills develop, a teacher will find that he or she will be able to chart several items during one listening session.

Step 3 (Charting) Figure 5.2 shows a form for recording teacher/instructional language. It lists categories for discrete listening.

Analysis

The information collected in a sample enables the teacher to formulate hypotheses concerning the possible effect on the student's performance. However, remember that this is only part of the interactive process. Analysis and hypothesis formulation must be completed on the other two sections of the basic triad (language content/concepts and student language) before intervention can take place.

Question Hierarchy

How to Ask Good Questions.
Some of the elements which make a good question are: precision, clarity, and close connection to the matters on which the question is based. Good questions recognize the wide possibilities of thought and are built around varying forms of thinking. They are directed toward learning and evaluative thinking rather than determining what has been learned in a narrow sense (Sanders, 1966, p. ix).

The question enables the teacher to control the quality and direction of the dialogue (Shrable and Minnis, 1969). Thus, the teacher's question-asking ability can extend a student's thinking and increase his or her ability to solve the problem.

---

1. *Expectation*
Was your expectation for this task understood by the student?
Yes _____ No _____

2. *Speaking mode*
Rate: Fast _____ Slow _____ Adequate _____
Amount: Estimate percentage of talking time _____

3. *Instructional mode*
a. Questions: How many questions were asked? _____
How many were narrow? _____ Broad? _____
What question words were used? _____
How many were repeated? _____
b. Directions: How many directions were given? _____
How many were single concept directions? _____
How many were multiple concept directions? _____
c. Explanations: Were explanations too long?
Yes _____ No _____
Were multiple concepts expressed in the directions?
Yes _____ No _____ How many? _____

4. *Syntactical mode*
a. Syntax: Simple sentences _____
Complex sentences _____
b. Length: How many complex sentences used in the direction and/or explanation?
_____

5. *Hypotheses*

Figure 5.2 Recording form for teacher/instructional language.

According to Bloom (1956) and Sanders (1966), questions can be organized on a hierarchy as follows:

Memory

Translation

Interpretation

Application

Analysis

Synthesis

Evaluation

(For a complete summary on the question hierarchy, see Table 5.1.) The hierarchy progresses from low level (concrete thinking requirements) to high level (abstract thinking skills). It can serve as a guide for teachers who wish to improve both their teaching and the student's learning.

Memory Memory questions require students to recall or recognize information previously presented to them. Students are *not* asked to compare or relate facts but rather to repeat them. Questions at this, the lowest level of thinking, are easy for the teacher to construct and thus are the most common form of question asked in the classroom. Unfortunately, the student's intellectual progress is limited to the accuracy and completeness of the teacher's information (Torrance and Myers, 1973). The responsibility for student learning is on the teacher. Because all content is

Table 5.1 *Summary of Question Levels*

Question level	Brief description	Key words	Reading[a]
Memory	Recall or recognition of facts	*Who, what, where, when* *How many* *Is, are, were* *Why*	Read the line
Translation	Change information into another symbolic form	*Retell* *Draw a picture*	Read the line
Interpretation	Discover relationships	*Compare/contrast* *What reason/evidence* *Describe* *Rearrange events*	Read between the lines
Application	Solve life-like problems using known information (only one answer is correct)	*What would happen if* *What other reasons* *What would you do if* *Compute . . .* *How does . . . affect*	Read between the lines
Analysis	Give reasons based on parts	*What will happen* *What is the purpose* *Find evidence* *Why* *Conclude*	Read beyond the lines
Synthesis	Use imagination to solve the problem	*What would you do if* *Pretend* *What ways might* *Develop a story* *Hypothesize*	Read beyond the lines
Evaluation	Establish standards and determine how ideas meet them	*Should* *Justify your choice* *Do you agree . . . . Why*	Read beyond the lines

Adapted from Meehan, 1970.
[a] This column refers to the question level.

given within the question, the student's only responsibility is to supply the one correct answer. This one-word response generally falls into a yes/no answer or the recall of a specific date, person, or place (i.e., *what, who* and *where*).

Some key phrases used in memory questions are:

Who was	*Find what . . . says to*
Who said	*Is*
What is (name, define)	*Are*
Can you	*Were*
When did	*List the*
How many	*Where did*

The reader may conclude that it is undesirable to ask a memory question. This is not intended. The reader must select the type of question that will produce the desired response and not fixate at the memory level.

Translation In the translation question, the student is asked to change information into a different symbolic form. Thus, the student might draw a picture of a story that has been read or heard or develop a play from such a story. The student might also match paraphrased sentences to those from the text, particularly when asked to show an understanding of metaphors or similes. At this level of thinking, the student is still not required to discover intricate relationships, implications, or subtle meanings but is required to give information in a different form.

Some key phrases used in translation questions include:

Briefly retell

Draw a picture to show

What does . . . mean

Tell me in your own words

Interpretation In moving to a third level of thinking, the student is asked to discover relationships. Such relationships may be among facts, generalizations, definitions, values, or skills. Thus, a student may be asked to determine if ideas are identical, similar, different, unrelated, or contradictory. In each case, however,

the teacher supplies the specific standards upon which such decisions are made.

In using interpretive questions, teachers often give their students an inductive conclusion and ask them to find evidence to support it. On the other hand, students might be asked to draw conclusions by looking at statistical information, such as graphs and charts.

In discussing the interpretative question, Sanders (1966) focused on question format in addition to cognitive process. He pointed out that *analogy questions* require the use of inference in a specific pattern; thus, "finger is to glove as ___ is to shoe." He suggested that teachers make the more general class into the unknown and that they ask their students to identify the relationship as part of the answer.

A second format within the interpretative question is the *irrelevant item question*. Here, the teacher gives the student a choice of three or four answers. All but one answer are correct. The student is expected to reason which one does not belong and why. The third format suggested by Sanders (1966) is that of the *scrambled outline*. Here, the student selects the main ideas and then organizes the related subheadings into a unified whole.

Some key phrases at this level include:

What can you conclude	*Interpret*
If it . . . then what	*Explain*
What reason or evidence	*Describe*
Rearrange these events	*Compare*

Application At the application level, the student is asked to solve a problem in the approximate form and context that he or she might encounter in a life situation. Thus, application questions really give the student practice in transfer of training. These questions are often characterized by giving minimal directions and instructions, by dealing with whole ideas and skills rather than with parts, and by showing that the student's knowledge has explanatory or problem-solving power (Sanders, 1966). For the first time, the student is asked to react to ideas and read between the lines (Meehan, Sr., 1970).

At this level, the student is expected to produce longer answers. In order to do this, more time is needed for the student to organize his or her thoughts. Thus, teachers using questions from this level on up the thinking ladder will find that the *time between questions increases while the number of questions decreases.*

Questions at this level begin with the following phrases:

What would you do if this happened to you

How does . . . affect

What do you suppose would happen if

What might they do with

What other possible reasons

If you know A and B, how could you determine C?

Analysis   The analysis question encourages orderly thinking whereby students must give *reasons based on their knowledge of parts.* In other words, students are required to take apart information and make relations by discovering the hidden meaning or reading between the lines.

Some teachers give their students examples of specific parts and ask them to inductively develop the generalization or the characteristics common to the entire class. On the other hand, other teachers give their students the generalization and ask them to deductively arrive at specific instances. This requires the use of inferences and syllogisms—items not frequently taught, even at the high school level. As might be concluded, this level of question is potentially one of the most important. However, the caution expressed by Torrance and Myers (1973) is well-taken—without sufficient training, analysis questions can be frustrating, and too many of them can become a tedious task.

Among the key phrases at the analysis level teachers would use are the following phrases:

Do you think he is

What do you think will happen

What is the author's purpose

Why

Would you

What way

Does that follow

Which are fact

What must you know for that to be true

Assumptions

Implications

Synthesis   Synthesis questions encourage students to do imaginative thinking in order to solve a problem. Thus, a student is asked to take elements from many different sources and put them together into a pattern that was not clearly there before. It is a drawing together (synthesizing) of information. Sanders (1966) felt that this particular question is tied more to an atmosphere than to a specific question form. The atmosphere he referred to is one of openness and freedom. It is one in which the student is encouraged to be unique and original, and it is one where many answers are possible.

Key words here include:

What ways . . . might

. . . could

. . . may

What if

What sort of

If no one else knew, how could you find out

Can you develop a new way

Think of a title to the story

What would you do if

Hypothesize

Predict

Summarize

Infer

Evaluation   The evaluation category is really a floating category because it is used at each level. At its most sophisticated level, however, the evaluation question asks the student to do two things: (1) to establish appropriate standards or values; and (2) to determine how closely his or her ideas or objectives meet these standards.

Teachers are cautioned against an evaluation question that calls for a *yes* or *no* response. For example, the question, "Are you enjoying the book?" requires a mere yes or no. What has it told the teacher about the student's ability to interact with the printed word or the characters in the story?

In contrast, Torrance and Myers (1973) noted

that the wise teacher does not comment on evaluation questions. Pupils' responses should not be rejected; teachers must withhold judgment so that pupils will discover they, too, have worthwhile ideas. Because this amount of freedom often is a new experience for students, teachers should be prepared for silliness and/or students who are upset because of the lack of ground rules. Needless to say, the transition is a planned event, not an automatic one.

Phrases that commonly occur in evaluative questions are:

Could

Should

What is your personal relation

How would you evaluate

Do you think

Justify your choice

Defend a position

For what reason would you favor

Which of . . . would you consider of greater value

Do you agree

Summary

When students experience problems in instructional tasks, teachers often assume that the problem lies within the student, e.g., lack of ability, poor motivation, or difficulty in attending to or following directions. This chapter directs attention to the importance of teacher language and its effect and relationship to the instructional task. Indeed, students' problems may be directly or indirectly related to the language of the teacher and the curriculum.

Teachers must learn to listen to themselves as well as examine the language expressed in curricular materials.

The information that this chapter provides hopefully will revise the teacher's perception of the effect of his or her language in the teaching and learning process.

Review Exercises

This review is designed to help the reader apply the principles discussed in this chapter to examples adapted from instructional tasks.

Following are types of questions a teacher may ask during an instructional day. Identify the appropriate type of question for each example.

Types of cognitive questions

Memory question

Translation question

Interpretation question

Application question

Analysis question

Synthesis question

Evaluation question

1. How long can the men stay under water? _____

2. Compare the standings of the Brewers to the standings of the White Sox. _____

3. Why are men in Hawaii testing machines? _____

4. How much will you save by buying a TV from a discount house instead of from a department store? _____

5. Think of a title for the story. _____

6. What can you conclude from the fact that Sara left the party? _____

7. How would you explain the worldwide interest in Elizabeth Taylor's 50th birthday? _____

8. Draw a picture of how John escaped from the jail. _____

9. Finger is to glove as _____ is to shoe. _____

10. Prepare a graph that plots each team's winnings within its league. _____

11. What would happen if we got 6 inches of rain this afternoon? _____

12. Do you agree with Susan's ideas about the antinuclear demonstration? Why? Why not? _____

13. Pretend you are a giraffe and write a story telling another giraffe about your adventure. _____

14. What evidence can you find to support the idea that John, the boy in the story, is worried? _____

Answers

1. memory
2. interpretation
3. memory
4. application
5. synthesis
6. analysis
7. evaluation
8. translation
9. interpretation
10. translation
11. application
12. evaluation
13. synthesis
14. analysis

List the concept words in this teacher direction and question.

Put your finger under the next word beside the picture that shows the front of the girl. What do you think the word is? Is there another arm besides the one that is labeled?

How would you rephrase this explanation?

Now we have put the members of the two sets together. This is the set of the ball and the block. The set of the ball put together with the set of the block is equal to the set of the ball and the block.

References

Amidon, J., and Flanders, N. 1967. The Role of a Teacher in the Classroom. Assoc. for Productive Teaching, Inc., Minneapolis.

Barnes, Douglas, 1971. Classroom context for language and learning Educ. Rev. June, 23:235–247.

Bartolome, P. I. 1969. Teachers' objectives and questions in primary reading. Read. Teach., 23:27–33.

Bloom, B. S. (ed.) 1956. Taxonomy of Educational Objectives: The Classification of Educational Goals, Handbook I, Cognitive Development. Longman, Inc. NY.

Bellack, A. A., Kliebard, H. M., Hyman, R. T., and

Smith, S. L. 1966. The Language of the Classroom. Teacher's College Press, New York.

Berlin, L., Blank, M., and Rose, S. 1980. Language of instruction: The hidden complexities. Top. Lang. Disord. 1:47–58.

Carin, A., and Sund, R. 1971. Developing Questioning Techniques: A Self-Concept Approach. Charles E. Merrill Publishing Co., Columbus, OH.

Cole, R. A., and Williams, D. M. 1973. Pupil response to teacher questions: Cognitive level, length and syntax. Educ. Lead. Res. Suppl. 142–145.

Cunningham, R. 1971. Developing question asking skills. In: N. J. Weigand (ed.), Developing Teacher Competencies. Prentice-Hall, Inc., Englewood Cliffs, NJ.

Dunkin, M., and B. Biddle, 1974. The Study of Teaching. Holt, Rinehart, Winston, Inc., New York.

Floyd, W. C. 1960. An analysis of the oral questioning activity in selected Colorado primary classrooms. Unpublished doctoral dissertation, Colorado State College, Greeley.

Foresman, S. 1971. Scott Foresman Reading Series, Scott, Foresman and Co., Glenview, IL.

Gall, M. D. 1970. The use of questions in teaching. J. Ed. Res. 40:707–720.

Guszak, F. J. 1967. Teacher questioning and reading. Read. Teach. 21:227–234.

Hunkins, F. 1976. Involving Students in Questioning. Allyn and Bacon, Inc., Boston.

Meehan, Sr., T. 1970. Critical reading and teachers' questions in theory and practice. Occasional Papers in Reading, Vol. III, May, 1970. (Bloomington, Indiana).

Melnik, A. 1968. Questions: An instructional-diagnostic tool. J. Read., 11:509–512, 578–581.

Minnis, D. L., and Shrabel, K. 1970. Teacher's Manual Proving Questioning Strategies. Search Models Unltd., San Arselmo, CA.

Pollak, S., and Gruenewald, L. 1978. A Manual for Assessing Language Interaction in Academic Tasks. Midwest IGE Services, Univ. of Wisconsin, Madison.

Rogers, V. M. 1972. Modifying questioning strategies of teachers. J. Teach. Educ. 23:58–62.

Rowe, M. B. 1969. Science, silence, and sanctions. Sci. Child. 6:11–13.

Sanders, N. 1966. Classroom Questions, What Kinds? Harper and Row, New York.

Shrabel, K., and Minnis, D. 1969. Interacting in the interrogative. J. Teach. Educ. 20:201–212.

Suppes, P., and Suppes, J. 1968. Sets and Numbers: K. Singer Mathematics Program. Singer Co., New York.

Taba, H. 1967. Teachers' Handbook for Elementary Social Studies. Addison-Wesley Publishing Co., Reading, MA.

Torrance, E. P., and Myers, R. E. 1973. Creative Learning and Teaching. Dodd, Meade and Co., New York.

Weigand, J. (ed.) 1971. Developing Teacher Competencies. Prentice-Hall, Inc., Englewood Cliffs, NJ.

Weigand, J. (ed.) 1977. Teacher Competencies—Positive Approaches to Personalizing Education. Prentice-Hall, Inc., Englewood Cliffs, NJ.

Yanicke, Georgia, 1975. An exploratory study on student teacher and pupil question asking behavior in the learning disabilities classroom. Unpublished doctoral dissertation, University of Wisconsin, Madison.

Suggested Readings

Dunkin, M., Biddle, B. 1974. The Study of Teaching. Holt, Rinehart, Winston, Inc., New York.
This reference book on teaching presents information relative to the methods, concepts, and findings of observational research on teaching.

Farley, G. T., and Clegg, A. A., Jr. 1969. Increasing the cognitive level of classroom questions in social studies: An application of Bloom's taxonomy. Paper presented as part of a symposium on Research in Social Studies Education at the Annual Convention of the American Educational Research Association, February 8, Los Angeles, CA.

Sanders, N. 1966. Classroom Questions, What Kinds? Harper and Row, New York.
This book focuses on eight basic types of questions to enhance students levels of thinking and expression. The information is directly applicable to all classroom teachers to help them become more aware of how their language of questions influences the students' thinking and language.

Torrance, E. P., and Myers, R. E. 1973. Creative Learning and Teaching. Dodd, Mead and Co., New York.
This book is designed to help educators become more aware of the relationship of teaching/learning and creative process. Several chapters focus on question-asking behavior of teachers.

Weigand, J. (ed.) 1971. Developing Teacher Competencies. Prentice-Hall, Inc., Englewood Cliffs, New Jersey.
This practical book for teachers covers seven different competency areas of instructional strategies. It is a self-study, designed to increase teaching skills in assessment, question asking, developing objectives, sequencing of instructions, and evaluation of programs.

Chapter 6
Student Language

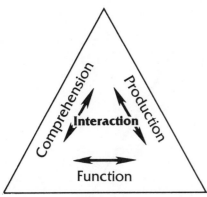

This chapter emphasizes the responsibility of the teacher to become a discrete listener of how the student produces language for academic use. It provides information that the teacher needs to know in order to assess the level of student language as required by the demands of the instructional task.

GOALS

1. To describe comprehension, production, and function of student language.
2. To provide developmental data concerning student language.
3. To alert the teacher of the relationship of student language to instruction.
4. To provide inventories for recording elements of student language.

In order to be successful in using language as a tool for learning, the student must first meet the following requirements (Yoder and Miller, 1972):

1. The student must have something to say (*language content/comprehension*)

2. He or she must have a way of saying it (*production*)

3. He or she must have a reason for saying it (*function*)
(See Figure 6.1)

The information that the teacher possesses about the student's language often is obtained through the language arts curriculum, which includes grammar, spelling, writing, and reading. However, to understand how student language interacts with the instructional task, the teacher must view it from a different perspective—that of comprehension, production, and use.

Although it is always desirable for the teacher to have as much theoretical information about

student language as possible, this may not be practical. A more realistic goal for the teacher would be to obtain information about student language that can be used to help solve problems in learning. In line with the stated objective of this book, this means that in a specific instructional task, the teacher would need to determine:

1. Whether the student has the comprehension of the language in the task

2. Whether the student has sufficient oral language to do the written language (reading and writing)

3. Whether the teacher is using language (oral and written) comparable to the student's comprehension

Why Is Information on Student Language Important to the Teacher?

Problems that a student encounters when learning academic subjects may be attributed to his or her inability to comprehend, produce, and

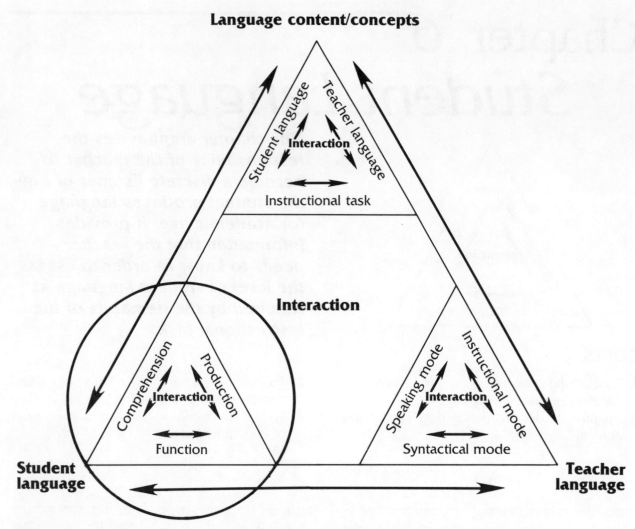

Figure 6.1 Student language in the expanded triad.

use language competently to learn a particular task. This use of language is very specific. The student may be able to communicate information, emotions, and needs in a social context but not be able to use this language for academic learning.

Students in regular education as well as those in special education often exhibit learning difficulties that have underlying problems in the comprehension, production, and use of language. If the teacher has information about how the student acquires, uses, and applies language to the instructional task, he or she may be able to intervene without supportive help. Some students, however, require specialized intervention by other professionals for their language-related learning problem. These professionals and the classroom teacher must work as a team so that intervention strategies for language can be integrated into the curricular tasks. Such interven-

tion can be carried out in self-contained and/or resource programs.

The classroom teacher has the best opportunity to observe the students' comprehension and use of language in learning and thus is the logical person to do the initial analysis and intervention of student language in the curricular task.

What Information Is Required about Student Language?

The teacher benefits from learning about:

1. Function (or use)

2. Comprehension

3. Production (phonology, major sentence structures, and constituent parts)

First, the teacher must be cognizant of the progressive nature of language development. This will help him or her to judge whether the student has acquired the language to do the task. It is inappropriate to ask the majority of students to use written language (reading and writing) before they have had the prerequisite experiences (cognitively and expressively) in oral, signing, and other forms of augmented communication.

The comprehension and use of language develops gradually in stages. In fact, the development and use of language can be looked at in terms of a hierarchy in academic learning—comprehension generally precedes speaking (oral production), which in turn precedes reading and writing.

To illustrate this hierarchy is a composition by a boy, 9 years of age, in a regular fourth-grade class. He was asked to write a story about Halloween and submitted the following:

> There were too good devils and too whch and double Frankenstein and there saw 3 boys and 2 girls and there run away then saw 4 boys and 1 girl and then there run in the manten (mountain) of the Pack and aren (cavern). The End

According to the teacher, the student's reading ability was 2 years below grade level, and his oral language (production) was considerably delayed. The teacher did not realize the significance of this oral language delay because the language responses required in classroom tasks were single words or short phrases. The teacher's approach to intervention included more practice in phonic skills, and the need for practice in oral language was disregarded.

Until teachers understand the hierarchy of language development (comprehension, speaking, reading, and writing), they will have difficulty knowing where and how to intervene. More practice in reading and writing is not indicated unless it is included as part of a total oral, as well as written, language program. Opportunities to practice and use oral language are always present in the meaningful context of the classroom.

Function (Pragmatics or Use)

Pragmatics is the subject of much current interest, and many professionals are concerned with assessing student language in pragmatic terms (i.e., the student's use of language in the context in which it occurs). This refers to the interaction of language between the speaker and listener within the environment and "includes social interactions, bodily movements, gestures and facial expression" (Geffner, 1981, p. 7). In the assessment of language interaction being discussed, pragmatics refers to the way students *use language in academic tasks* rather than how they produce it in a social situation. For the student to use language meaningfully within instructional contexts requires skills and knowledge about the semantic and syntactic features of the language. This meaning is derived from the acquisition of concepts, which also underlies production and use of language. A discussion of meaning (semantics) is difficult because of its elusive nature and "because it overlaps so generously with both syntax and pragmatics (function)" (Miller, 1981, p. 41). When the student cannot comply with the expectations of the teacher or the demands of the task (pragmatics), one of the reasons may be that he or she does not have the language skills (semantics, syntactics) for use in the context of a *specific instructional task*.

Within the instructional context, it is the role of the teacher to help students formulate ideas, discover relationships, verbalize their experiences, and to consider the viewpoints of other persons. Teachers should encourage the use of oral language for these purposes in order for the student to develop it as a tool for learning (Olswang et al., 1982).

Tough (1977a, pp. 82–86) categorized the use of language in elementary classroom into seven areas.

Category	Language used
Self-maintaining (justifying behavior)	"I'm hitting him because he spoiled my picture."
Directing (collaborating in action with others)	"You cut the paper and I'll stick it and we'll put it on there for an airplane."
Reporting (referring to detail)	"That little red bus has a door at the back that opens."

Category	Language used
Toward logical reasoning (recognizing causal and dependent relationships)	"If the bridge is low, boats can't go under and it will have to open in the middle to let them go through."
Predicting (predicting consequences of actions or events)	"That propeller will fall off if you can't stick it on properly."
Projecting (projecting into the experiences of others)	"He's driving fast in his car and it'll be all windy and cold, and he hasn't got a coat on."
Imagining	"The little boy wanted his mommy, but the bad boys took him, and he was frightened and he cried."

It is interesting to note that the language used in each of the seven categories is comprised of simple, compound, and complex sentences. The use and meaning are always interdependent, and both are dependent on comprehension. The teacher can obtain information about student language use by completing the suggested Language Use Inventory in Figure 6.2.

Comprehension

Comprehension underlies the production of both oral and written language. Indeed, a student can produce language without comprehension, but this stereotypic or automatic production of language cannot be used for learning academics. Similarly, language can be produced with a need for a particular function but again, this language cannot be used as a tool for learning. To be used as a tool for learning, language must be meaningful in the context of academic learning. Not only does the student have to understand the meaning (semantics) of single words but he or she must also understand the meaning of simple words within different sentence constructions (simple, compound, and complex).

The student's ability to understand complex sentences is as crucial to reading and mathe-

matics as it is to listening (Stark, 1981). This requirement is exemplified in mathematics, where story and word problems require comprehension of the syntactic rules of grammar. For example:

> The empty set in union with the set whose member is the rabbit is equal to the set whose member is the rabbit. (Suppes and Suppes, 1968).

The complex sentence structure may obscure the math problem. The teacher needs to know whether the student understands and uses complex sentences. If the student cannot understand the complex sentence, can he understand compound or simple sentence?

Likewise, the same interference with learning applies to reading comprehension. Reading texts that have a high interest level and low vocabulary level are sometimes chosen for upper elementary-age and adolescent handicapped students. This may be appropriate. What may *not* be appropriate is the high skill level required by the student in using complex sentences demanded by these texts. The handicapped student may not be able to comprehend or use these complex sentences orally, let alone in the reading assignment.

A summary of a story used in a reading lesson for a class of mildly retarded children, 10 years of age, illustrates some of these points. The specific task of the lesson was to check comprehension by having the teacher ask questions about the following story, which the students had just read. This task required knowledge of the facts and the order in which they occurred as well as vocabulary comprehension and use.

Story

Jimmy and his sister wanted to make a garden in the spring so they went down to the store and bought some seeds. On the way back, they rested on a bench in the park and when they arrived home, they found that Jimmy had lost the seeds through a hole in his pocket. During the summer Jimmy and his sister decided to have a picnic, and his sister decided to pack a lunch. They went to the park. Suddenly they saw a little patch of flowers near the bench on which they had rested in the spring. Jimmy was sure that the seeds he had lost had blossomed into these flowers and that they had their little garden after all.

Teacher: Mary, can you tell us the story that we just read?

Mary: Jimmy going to make a garden—plant some seeds.

Teacher: Okay.

Mary: And he dropped them on the way to the picnic. He dropped them. They had lunches packed for the picnic.

Teacher: Hmmmmmm.

Mary: They went to the park and eat their lunch.

Teacher: Hmmmmmm.

Mary: *They packed lunches.*

Teacher: Hmmmmmm.

Mary: They went walking to the park and he lost them on the way.

Analysis Mary's responses provide information about her ability to comprehend the story as well as the teacher's questions.

1. She did not comprehend the main idea.

2. She did not have sufficient language to translate the story into her own words.

3. The type of sentences used were simple and compound.

4. Problems existed in sequencing and ordering.

This information will lead to several hypotheses:

Hypothesis 1 Mary may not comprehend complex sentences.

Hypothesis 2 Mary may not comprehend cause-and-effect relationships.

Hypothesis 3 Mary may not comprehend sequential order of the events.

Teachers sometimes regard recall as a sign of comprehension. Reading assignments usually include questions that require recall of one or more events. This may be regarded as comprehension of the question asked but not necessarily comprehension of the story. Comprehension of the story requires the student to put the meaning of the main idea of the story into his or her own words or in a different representational form (picture or role play). The most usual form for communicating meaning in instructional tasks is through oral or written sentences. The students' acquisition of comprehension and use of vocabulary and sentence structure is based on a developmental progression.

To comprehend oral and written language, the student must not only understand the vocabulary but also the meaning within simple, compound, or complex sentences. The teacher will be able to analyze the student's ability to comprehend if he or she knows how to examine the major sentence structures and their constituent parts.

Production (Syntax)

Phonology

Phonology refers to the sound system. There is a developmental progression in acquiring the sounds of language. Figure 6.2 shows a general inventory of phonology, which serves as a guide to indicate the sequence in which sounds usually appear. If a student has learned the sounds by these ages, his or her speech is developing normally. However, many students master these sounds before the period indicated.

A student should have acquired the use of all the sounds in the English language by the time he or she is 7 or 8 years of age. Students who omit, substitute, or distort sounds or words exhibit articulation problems. By referring to the inventory of phonology, the teacher is able to determine whether the student exhibits a significant delay in producing sounds for a child of his or her chronologic age.

The omission of the sound /s/ at the end of the word may not be an articulation problem at all. The student may omit the final /s/ because he or she does not know the appropriate construction for its use, i.e., in plurals and possessives. This omission or inconsistent use of final /s/ in the syntactical sense is very often observed in hearing-impaired, mildly retarded, language-disordered, or learning-disabled students. These students may not have developed the sound, but on the other hand, it must be ascertained whether the student is capable of producing it but does not use it. The reason for this might be the lack of the concept (meaning) of plurality or possessives, which is marked by the phoneme /s/. Third person singular could be another instance of omission of /s/ attributable to the lack of temporal concept development.

Speech and language clinicians may provide consultation to the teacher or may intervene directly with students who demonstrate delays or disorders in articulation.

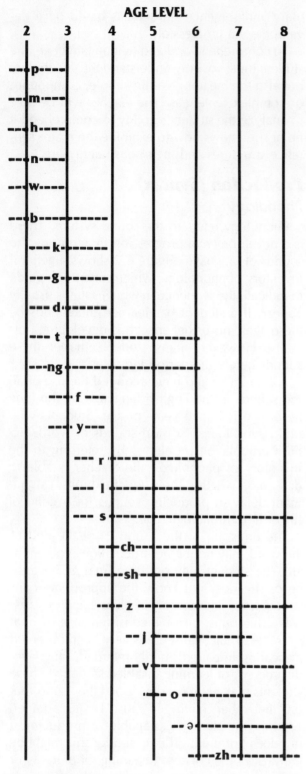

AGE LEVEL

Figure 6.2 Inventory of phonology (Sanders, 1972). Average age estimates and upper age limits of customary consonant production are shown. The solid bar corresponding to each sound starts at the median age of customary articulation and stops at the age level at which 90% of all children are customarily producing the sound.

Major Sentence Structures

Students usually enter school with the ability to combine words into phrases, clauses, and sentences. The student's development of syntax shows considerable expansion during the elementary school years. Kean and Personke (1976) stated that teachers need to be familiar with the syntax system that students bring to school and also with the developmental changes that occur during the elementary school years.

Students use sentences by imitating adults in specific situations. This does not guarantee that they comprehend what they are saying or that they will be able to generalize the use of these sentences to other situations. Teachers are sometimes misled into assuming that because a student uses appropriate *social* language, he or she can use this social language for academic purposes. This is especially true with mentally retarded as well as learning-disabled students. To use language for learning and problem solving requires comprehension of not only the meaning of sentences but also the rules that generate them.

Major sentence structures include:

1. The simple sentence, which consists of subject, verb, and object, e.g. "The boy went to the store," or "The boy bought candy."

2. The compound sentence, which consists of two simple sentences joined by a conjunction, e.g., "The boy went to the store and the boy bought candy."

3. The complex sentence, which is comprised of one or more independent clauses and one or more dependent clauses connected by a subordinate conjunction. The subordinate conjunction may or may not be stated in the sentence. When it is not stated, it is considered embedded, e.g., "The boy who went to the store bought candy."

Sentence complexity does not imply obscure meaning but rather refers to the normal development in oral and written language (Loban, 1976).

The use of complex language structure also parallels the ability to use cognitive structures. For example, to say, *The large brown flat envelope was lost when the wind scattered the papers* requires not only the ability to use a *dependent clause* but also the ability to use language describing the attributes of the envelope.

The child has to develop the major sentence structures of English and has to order the relationships of the parts of speech with those major structures. How these parts of speech are used determines the complexity of clauses and sentences. It must always be kept in mind that meaning underlies the use of the sentence.

The comprehension and production of simple, compound, and complex sentences develops gradually. Loban (1976) cautioned that displaying a developmental chart is difficult because student language ability varies greatly. However, in spite of this caution, an adaptation of Loban's chart is included (see Table 6.1) because it provides information that classroom teachers need concerning the progressive nature of major sentence structure. These developmental milestones serve as a reference for the teacher to compare the student's language production of sentences with that of most children at the same age level. It also serves as a guide for formulating questions about student language readiness for the task.

Table 6.1 *Developmental milestones (major sentence structures)[a]*

Ages 5 and 6	Children consistently use pronouns and verbs in the present and past tenses. Complex sentences appear frequently. Conditionality (*You eat your dinner, you have banana.*) and causality (*Don't sit on 'at radiator—very hot.*) expressed by *why, because,* and *if* are implicit in the children's language. The average number of words per communication unit will be about 6.8.[a]
Ages 6 and 7	Further progress in complex sentences, especially those with adjectival clauses. Conditional dependent clauses, such as those beginning with *if* appear. The average number of words per oral communication unit will be about 7.5 with a variation between 6.6 and 8.1.[a]
Ages 7 and 8	Children can now use relative pronouns as objects in subordinate adjectival clauses (I have a cat *which* I feed every day). Subordinate clauses beginning with *when, if,* and *because* appear frequently. The gerund phrase as an object of a verb appears (*I like washing myself*). The average number of words per communication unit in oral language will be about 7.6.[b]
Ages 8, 9 and 10	Children begin to relate particular concepts to general ideas, using such connectors as *meanwhile, unless, even if.* About 50% of the children begin to use the subordinating connector *although* correctly. They begin to use the present participle active: *Sitting up in bed, I looked around.* The perfect participle appears: *Having read Tom Sawyer, I returned it to the library.* The gerund as the object of a preposition appears: *By seeing the movie, I didn't have to read the book.* *The average number of words per communication unit in oral language will be 9 with a variation from 7.5 to 9.3.*[a]
Ages 10, 11 and 12	At this age, children form hypotheses and envision their consequences. This involves using complex sentences with subordinate clauses introduced by connectives like *provided that, nevertheless, in spite of,* and *unless.* Auxiliary verbs such as *might, could,* and *should* will appear more frequently than at earlier stages of language development. They have difficulties in distinguishing and using the past, past perfect, and present perfect tenses of the verb, and almost none of them use the expanded forms of the past perfect or the future perfect. The stage of thinking *if this, then (probably) that* is emerging, usually applied to temporal things rather than to nontemporal ideas and relations. *If the cost of higher education escalates, then (probably) enrollment will falter.* The average number of words per spoken communication unit will be about 9.5, with a variation from 8 to 10.5.[a] The average number per written unit in the study was 9 with a range from 6.2 to 10.2, depending upon the child's verbal proficiency.

Adapted from Loban, 1976, pp. 81–84.

[a] A communication unit may be defined as a group of words that cannot be further divided without a loss of their essential meaning (Loban, 1976, p. 105). In Loban's research, this communication unit generally appeared to be comprised of an independent clause with its modifiers.

Implications for Instruction   An example selected from a sixth-grade social studies text (Binder, 1976) demonstrates the semantic and syntactic demands placed upon the student in reading in content areas. The task may need to be modified so that it is commensurate with the level of comprehension of the student.

> The fights which were carried on from time to time between various tribes . . . can hardly be called "wars" because all fights were in the nature of armed raids. For example, when cattle disease invaded the Masai country and reduced their livestock below the minimum, the Masai, whose lives depended entirely on meat, milk, and blood of animals, were forced by necessity to raid the stock of their neighbors or die of hunger and starvation (p. 327).

Analysis of Sentence Structure   The complex sentence structure contains many independent and dependent clauses. Also, the words *nature* and *stock* have double meanings.

Hypothesis 1   The student may not understand extended sentence complexity (many dependent clauses)

Hypothesis 2   The student may not understand the double meaning of words *nature* and *stock*.

Analyzing the language demands of this example for the student who has difficulty with the task might result in the following revision:

From time to time represents time duration (see Chapter 3) and it could be rewritten *for many years* if the student has difficulty with this concept.

Nature of armed raids requires understanding of double function meaning of *nature*. In rewriting, it could be deleted without loss of meaning.

Stock could be substituted by the word *animals* or *livestock*.

The complex syntax could be rewritten if the student has difficulty with complex sentences containing dependent clauses. A simpler syntactical form could be used, as follows:

> The fights, which were carried on for many years between various tribes, were armed raids rather than wars. For example, when cattle disease invaded the Masai country, it reduced their livestock so that there was not enough food. The Masai, whose lives depended entirely on the meat, milk, and blood of animals, were forced to raid the livestock of their neighbors or die of hunger or starvation.

Constituent Parts

With the development of complex sentences, there is a simultaneous growth of the constituent parts. Constituent parts can be defined as parts of speech and include:

Morphology	Other constituent parts
tenses	prepositions
plurals	conjunctions
possessives	negation
comparatives	questions
	modifiers (adjectives and adverbs)

For purposes of conciseness, several of these constituent parts are grouped together for explanation and analysis.

Because plurals, tenses, possessives, and comparatives have characteristics in common, they are grouped under the heading of morphology (see Table 6.2). Morphology refers to the small units of meaning that describe the word. Addition or deletion of this small unit results in a change of meaning of the word as in

Plurals— *-s*, meaning *more than one*

Tenses— *-ed*, meaning *past*

Comparatives— *-er* and *-est*, meaning *greater than*

Implications for Instruction (Morphology) Some errors in a student's use of word forms can be attributed to lack of development. Current notions concerning the student's acquisition of morphological rules (changes in word form) indicate that the student learns a rule system, rather than the correct words solely through imitation. This can easily be seen in a young student who uses a word or phrase, *I sawed Tommy do that.*

Table 6.2 *Developmental milestones (morphology)*

By age 4	Plural—Uses -*s* and -*z* but not consistently Tenses—Uses progressive (-*ing*); simple past (-*t* and -*d*) not consistent Progressives—My/mine emerging; uses nouns with final -*s*; *his, her* Comparatives—Not used
By age 5	Plurals—Uses -*s* and -*z* more consistently; -*es*, -*ez* not consistent Tenses—Simple past, future tense, and present progressive more consistent; *have* and *have not* not used Possessives—Use of -*s*, *my, mine,* and *more* consistent Comparatives—Not used
By age 6	Plurals—Uses -*es* and -*ez* more consistently; irregular form emerges Possessives—Uses correctly with greater consistency. Comparatives—Regular
By age 7 and 8	Plurals—Improves use of irregular form Tenses—*Have* and *had* developed Comparatives—Uses irregular correctly

He is trying to regularize a verb that is used as an irregular verb, indicating that the rule system has not yet been learned. It is important to build upon the student's early knowledge of morphology. Other errors may be attributed to hearing, which influences a student's ability to distinguish morphemes in the speech context. Attesting to this is the fact that hearing students score far above deaf students in tests of morphological ability, particularly with reference to more complex markers, such as derivational suffixes (Cooper, 1963).

Plurals and Possessives   Students may omit -*es* in plurals and possessives because they have acquired the use of the sound in their speech or the concept of plurality. Moreover, the endings -*ed* or -*ing* may be used incorrectly because the student may not have acquired the time concepts that underlie the use of that particular form.

Tenses   Teachers often are misled into assuming that because the student can use the correct endings and word form in *oral* production, he or she can comprehend and use them in written forms. This can be observed in the errors students often make in workbook exercises, where their directions are to fill in the blank from a choice of words. For example:

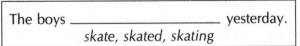

The boys _____ yesterday.
skate, skated, skating

The student may insert the incorrect word (e.g., *skating*) but upon reading the sentence *aloud*, will change to the correct word (*skated*).

This is attributable to what is called the *implicit* use of language. The student may not have the *explicit* use of language to do the written exercise. This explicit use requires that the student apply *rules* based on the understanding that changes in the form and word ending changes the meaning. This meaning involves the concept of temporality (past, present, future). If the student has not fully acquired the concept of temporality, then this may have important consequences for successfully learning many instructional tasks. Not only must the student have the concept of temporality in his or her oral speech, the student also must be able to generalize the concept to the written form. An example in context will clarify this point further.

In the following example, the students did a workbook activity that they previously had done orally with no difficulty. These students were 10 years of age in a learning disabilities class. The teacher chose this paper-and-pencil task to determine whether the students could use the correct endings of words in the *written* form. The exercise consisted of using morphological rules, i.e., changing word endings to denote tense change. All six students failed the written task. To determine whether the students understood that the changes in endings changed the meaning, the teacher wrote the words *jump, jumps, jumping* and *jumped* on the blackboard. The following exchange ensued:

Teacher: Do all these words mean the same thing, Susie?

Susie: No, they got all kinds of different words on the end.

Teacher: Okay, they have different endings. How does the ending change the meaning of the word?

Susie: Because like if you just say jump and jumps. Like jump means you jump high and you know jumps means you can jump more times.

(Is Susie confusing third person singular with plurality?)

Teacher: Steve, what about jumped? How is jumped different from jump? Brian, do you have any idea?

Students: No response.

Teacher: Susie:

Susie: You can jumps more than jump—you can jump even more times than jumped.

Additional exercises elicited the information that the students did not have the concept of temporality firmly established; therefore, they could not understand the meaning of the morphological changes.

The comprehension and use of *-ed* and *-ing* denoting temporality underlie the student's ability to sequence events and ideas and to relate these ideas in a logical fashion within a story. Unless students understand temporality in the written forms, they may have difficulty understanding the *sequences* of events in reading. They also may have trouble answering questions that deal with past, present, and future events in stories because they do not truly understand what the question requires. The implications in using temporal concepts are even greater when the middle school student is asked to read in content areas, such as science, history, and social studies and is expected to answer questions that involve time sequences.

In analyzing the relationship between comprehension and production and the concepts underlying the changes in word forms, the teacher may want to consider whether:

1. The students understand the *concepts* underlying the use of present, past, and future tenses

2. The students understand the concept of relationships underlying the use of *-er* and

-est in comparatives (see chapter 3 under seriation)

3. The students understand the concept of ownership underlying the use of possessives and the concept of *more than one* underlying the use of plurals

4. The students understand that the word endings change the meaning of a sentence

5. The students are able to use correct morphological endings in their oral and written language.

Implications for Instruction (Other Constituent Parts)

Prepositions Prepositions show the relationship between other words (see Table 6.3). By the time a student enters school, he or she is using a variety of prepositional phrases. Prepositions often are used to express spatial and temporal concepts. They are embedded in teacher instructions and academic tasks, particularly in kindergarten and first grade. Students often have difficulty in following directions. For example, in "Draw closed curves with the points *on inside and outside*," the three prepositions used are simple for a child, 6 years of age to understand. What is difficult is the ordered relationship in the complex direction.

Conjunctions The use of *and* between many words or unrelated phrases does not mean that the student is using a compound sentence, nor does it necessarily mean that this student has the concept of connecting two related sentences.

Athey (1977) reviewed research confirming that *and* is one of the easiest conjunctions to comprehend at the fourth-grade level. (The others are *how, for,* and *as*). The most difficult conjunctions are: *when, so, but, or, where, while,* and *if*. This could be attributed to the underlying concepts of causality (*or, if so*), temporal duration (*when, while*), and negation (*but*). The development of these concepts parallels the development of the complex sentence. The use of *and* in grouping objects and events is significant in math activities. For instance, when the student is asked to add "2 plus 2," the connector *and* is implied. If the student has difficulty with the concept of addition, the teacher may question whether he or she is able to use *and* in oral language in order to group objects.

Table 6.3 *Developmental milestones (other constituent parts)*

By age 4

Adjectives—Adjectives (*simple*) used
Adverbs—Abverbs of location (*there, here*) used
Pronouns—*I* and *me* inconsistent; *it*
Conjunctions—*And* used consistently to coordinate; *because* emerging; *if* and *so* not used
Negation—*Not, no, can't,* and *don't* used
Questions—Upward intonation at end of sentences; *what, what do* used
Prepositions—*In, on, with, of, for, to, up,* and *at* used

By age 5

Adjectives—Errors in agreement between adjective and noun
Adverbs—Adverbs of time and manner in addition to location
Pronouns—Consistently used; reflexive pronoun emerging
Conjunctions—*Because* used more consistently; *if* and *so* emerging
Questions—*Why* questions inconsistent; inversion of subject and auxiliary
Prepositions—*After, before, until, down, through, over, under,* and *near* used

By ages 6–7

Conjunctions—*But, after, before* (temporal), *if,* and *so* more consistently used; *because* and *therefore* used as *then* with no causal relationship
Pronouns—Reflexive pronoun used
Prepositions—Correctly used
Questions—*How* emerging

The language development inventory included in each section was constructed from several sources (Brown,1973; Loban, 1976; Miller, 1974; Nelson, 1976).

Negatives A child uses the words *no* and *not* at a very early age, which leads to an incorrect assumption that he or she has the concept of negation. The concept of negation expressed in the passive mode ("The ball was *not* hit by the girl") is more difficult to comprehend and produce than the simple declarative active mode ("The girl did not hit the ball"). Athey (1977) showed that students find it more difficult to identify an object that is square and not red than one that is square and red. Athey further stated that

> The negative connotations and opposition of ideas implied in the use of the word *but* seems to be quite

difficult for some children of elementary school age when confronted with a sentence such as: "One cannot always be a hero ___ one can always be a man" (p. 74). ". . . This item is a subtest of the Stanford-Binet and is placed at age 12 (p. 79).

Preschool, kindergarten, and first-grade students usually are taught *same* and *different.* In order for the student to use these terms, he or she must also know *not the same.* The *not* indicates a different class of objects. This is very important in learning how to group and classify sets and subsets. In subtraction activities, the student must learn to group and regroup. This involves the concept of *not* in a concrete task, which is a prerequisite to the abstract activity of subtraction.

Questions The student's comprehension and use of questions involves both concepts and structure. Preschool children (approximately 2–3 years of age) can comprehend *what, what doing, what is, where, what kind,* and *who* types of questions. These may be considered quite concrete or narrow questions. If a student seems to comprehend the questions, however, it does not necessarily follow that he or she can *use* the question form. The form may involve the inversion of the subject and verb. Question forms that begin with such words as *which, when, how,* and *why* develop at a later stage. If the student does not respond to a teacher's question, it should be determined if the student understands and uses that question word. For example, when a student does not respond to a *how* question, the teacher will automatically restate it using the *what* form. It would be revealing to a teacher to monitor the question form to determine the question words to which the student responds.

Table 6.4 outlines the student's development of *wh-* questions.

Student Language Analysis Guide

The Student Language Analysis Guide is designed to help the reader gain experience and practice in analyzing student language required in an instructional task.

Because of the complexity of listening to and recording student language, it is suggested that the reader confine his or her analysis to the language that is required by the task. This will include the curricular materials and teacher interaction.

Table 6.4 The student's development of wh- questions

Question form	Concept presented	Structure of response
What + be	Identity	Noun
What + do	Action	Verb
Where	Space	Adverb/prepositional phrase
What kind (color, shape, size)	Classification	Adjective to description
Who	People	Noun, pronoun
Whose	Possessive	Possessive
Why	Cause/effect	*Because* phrase
How	Manner/method	Adverb/adjective
Many/few	Number	
Much/little	Quantity	
Often/soon	Time	
Far/near	Distance	
Long/short	Linear measure of time	
Heavy/light	Weight	
Big/small	Size	
When	Time	Adverb/prepositional phrase/tense
Which	Selection/multiple choice	

Bellugi, 1965; Brown, 1968; Ervin-Tripp, 1970.

Student Language Analysis Guide

I. Major sentence structures required by the task
  A. Simple sentences _____
  B. Compound sentences _____
     (*and, but, or*)
  C. Complex sentences _____
     (*when, if, because*)

II. Constituent parts of the sentence structures
  A. Morphological endings
    Plurals: regular (*-s, -es*) _____
           irregular (*man/men*)_____

    Tenses: regular (*-ed, -t*) _____
           irregular (*went, run*)_____
    Possessives: _____
    Comparatives (*-er, -est*): _____

  B. Other constituent parts
    Prepositions: _____
    Conjunctions: _____
    Negation (*no, not*) _____
    Questions (*what, where,*
      who, when, how, which, why) _____
    Modifiers (*adjectives, adverbs*) _____

The information collected for the analysis of student language is incorporated in the summary analysis of language interaction (see Chapter 7) so that the hypotheses concerning the effects of the interacting components on the students' learning can be formed.

Student Language Use Inventory

The purpose of the Student Language Use Inventory (see Figure 6.3) is to record the student's use of language in the variety of structured and unstructured situations in the classroom and school environment. It will yield information that

I. Giving information
    1. Student gives information to others _____ often _____ only when asked ____ sometimes on his own _____ usually on his own.
    2. When talking and explaining things student uses _____ complete sentences _____ short phrases _____ single words.
    3. Student gives information _____ in classroom discussion _____ one-to-one conversation _____ play or free time with other students.
    4. The kind of information or talking the student usually does is to
       _____ talk/describe what he's doing
       _____ talk/describe what someone else is doing
       _____ name or describe things
       _____ tell what he is going to do
       _____ tell what he did or has done
       _____ tell about something (an event) that happened
       _____ explain why/why not he did something
       _____ tell what he needs or wants
       _____ tell how to do something
    5. When student gives information or explains something, people _____ usually understand _____ sometimes understand _____ have difficulty understanding.

II. Getting information
    1. Student gets most of his or her information (learns best) through: _____ listening __ seeing _____ reading _____ doing it himself _____ a combination of all of these.
    2. If student doesn't know something, _____ he or she usually asks _____ sometimes asks _____ rarely asks.

III. Self-expression
    1. Student uses language to ask permission.
    2. Student uses language to refuse to do something.
    3. Student uses language to criticize something/someone.
    4. Student uses language to praise something/someone.
    5. Student uses language to say what he believes.
    6. Student uses language to explain how he feels.
    7. Student uses language to say what he wants to do.

IV. Learning new things
    1. When learning something new, student practices it aloud.
    2. Student practices it silently to himself.
    3. Student practices it with a friend.

Figure 6.3 Language use inventory (adapted from Flood-Pauly, 1976).

Student Language Analysis Guide—Practice Exercise 1

I. Major sentence structures required by the task
   A. Simple sentences _____
   B. Compound sentences _____
       (*and, but, or*)
   C. Complex sentences _____
       (*when, if, because*)

II. Constituent parts of the sentence structures
   A. Morphological endings
       Plurals: regular (*-s, -es*) _____
                   irregular (*man/men*) _____

       Tenses: regular (*-ed, -t*) _____
                   irregular (*went, run*) _____
       Possessives: _____
       Comparatives (*-er, -est*): _____

   B. Other constituent parts
       Prepositions: _____
       Conjunctions: _____
       Negation (*no, not, but*) _____
       Questions (*what, where*)
          who, when, how, which, why) _____
       Modifiers (*adjectives, adverbs*) _____

---

is not tapped by the Student Language Analysis Guide, which is used to record the student language required by the task. The two forms yield important information about a student who is having difficulty with an academic task.

The Student Language Use Inventory can be used to obtain information gradually on the selected target student. Observations can be made one section at a time for a period of days or in a variety of situations.

Practice Exercises

Analyze the language demands of the following examples. Assume that the student is expressing difficulty in comprehending the written material. Use the Student Language Analysis Guides to record the sentence structure and constituent parts for each exercise.

Practice Exercise 1 (Grade 3)[1]

Suppose you buried your clay imprint when it dried. Suppose a million years from now, someone found it. Your imprint would be as hard as stone. It would be a fossil of your hand. It would tell something about you. It would tell the person who finds it something about life on earth a million years earlier.

Practice Exercise 2 (Grade 5)[2]

But I think that in losing those worldly possessions, they found themselves and they found that only through dedication to serving mankind—and in this case to serving the poor and those who are struggling for justice—only in that way could they find themselves.

---

[1] Adapted from Clymer and Venezky, 1982, p. 168.

[2] Adapted from Allen, 1979, p. 337.

Student Language Analysis Guide—Practice Exercise 2

I. Major sentence structures required by the
   task
   A. Simple sentences _____
   B. Compound sentences _____
      (and, but, or)
   C. Complex sentences _____
      (when, if, because)

II. Constituent parts of the sentence structures
   A. Morphological endings
     Plurals: regular (-s, -es) _____
               irregular (man/men)_____

     Tenses: regular (-ed, -t) _____
               irregular (went, run)_____
     Possessives: _____
     Comparatives (-er, -est): _____

   B. Other constituent parts
     Prepositions: _____
     Conjunctions: _____
     Negation (no, not, but) _____
     Questions (what, where,
       who, when, how, which, why) _____
     Modifiers (adjectives, adverbs) _____

Practice Exercise 3 (Grade 4)[3]

People all over the world learn by trial and error and by copying. But why do people behave in different ways in different places?

First, trial-and-error learning happens in different places with different materials. You might learn by yourself to peel the bark off an ubussu palm tree and eat the inside. But you could learn this only in a place where these palm trees grow. The Tasaday might learn by themselves to make a peanut butter and jelly sandwich. But they could learn this only where there are bread, peanut butter and jelly.

Second, people copy different people. You probably have never watched someone making fire with sticks. You did not learn that behavior because you did not have someone to copy. In the same way, the Tasaday have never watched anyone turning on a kitchen stove or unlocking a door.

Practice Exercise 4 (Grade 4)[4]

More than 3,700 years ago, a man named Hammurabi ruled the country that was then called Babylonia. In those days, the people had laws, but they were not the same throughout the land. In some places, business people were charging terribly high prices. Poor people were having to become slaves to the people to whom they owed money because they could never pay it back.

Hammurabi had a set of over 300 laws made up for his country. He had the laws written on a big block of black stone. This written *code*, or set of laws, was Hammurabi's most important gift to the world. Later, countries used Hammurabi's Code as the basis for their own laws (Paramore and D'Amelio, 1982, p. 220).

---

[3] Speas et al., 1979, p. 75. Reprinted from Studying Cultures, T. E. (Grade 4). by Speas, J., Ochoa, A., Cherryholmes, Co., and Manson, G., © 1979, with permission of Webster/McGraw-Hill.

[4] Adapted from Paramore and D'Amelio, 1982, p. 22.

Student Language Analysis Guide—Practice Exercise 3

I.   Major sentence structures required by the
     task
     A. Simple sentences   _____
     B. Compound sentences _____
         (and, but, or)
     C. Complex sentences   _____
         (when, if, because)

II. Constituent parts of the sentence structures
     A. Morphological endings
         Plurals: regular (-s, -es)   _____
                    irregular (man/men) _____

         Tenses: regular (-ed, -t)   _____
                    irregular (went, run)_____
         Possessives: _____
         Comparatives (-er, -est):   _____

     B. Other constituent parts
         Prepositions: _____
         Conjunctions: _____
         Negation (no, not, but)   _____
         Questions (what, where,
             who, when, how, which, why)   _____
         Modifiers (adjectives, adverbs)   _____

Student Language Analysis Guide—Practice Exercise 4

I.   Major sentence structures required by the
     task
     A. Simple sentences   _____
     B. Compound sentences _____
         (and, but, or)
     C. Complex sentences   _____
         (when, if, because)

II. Constituent parts of the sentence structures
     A. Morphological endings
         Plurals: regular (-s, -es)   _____
                    irregular (man/men) _____

         Tenses: regular (-ed, -t)   _____
                    irregular (went, run)_____
         Possessives: _____
         Comparatives (-er, -est):   _____

     B. Other constituent parts
         Prepositions: _____
         Conjunctions: _____
         Negation (no, not, but)   _____
         Questions (what, where,
             who, when, how, which, why)   _____
         Modifiers (adjectives, adverbs)   _____

References

Allen, J. 1979. Americans. American Book Co., New York.

Athey, I. 1977. Syntax, semantics and reading. In: J. T. Guthrie, Curriculum and Comprehension. International Reading Association, Newark, DE.

Bellugi, U. 1965. The development of interrogative structures in children's speech. In: K. F. Fiegel (ed.), The Development of Language Functions. Report #8, Center for Human Growth and Development, University of Michigan, Ann Arbor.

Brown, R. 1968. The development of questions in child speech. J. Verb. Learn. Verb. Behav. 7:279–290.

Brown, R. 1973. A First Language. Harvard University Press, MA.

Clymer, T., and Venezky, R. 1982. Ten Times Round, Level 10. Ginn and Co., Columbus, OH.

Cooper, R. 1963. The Ability of Deaf and Hearing Children to Apply Morphological Rules. Unpublished doctoral dissertation. Columbia University, 1963.

Ervin-Tripp, S. 1970. Discourse agreement: how children answer questions. In: J. Hayes (ed.), Cognition and the Development of Language. John Wiley and Sons, Inc., New York.

Flood-Pauley, C., 1976. Communicative Function Questionnaire. Unpublished.

Geffner, Donna, 1981. Assessment of language disorders: Linguistic and cognitive functions. Top. Lang. Disord., 1:3, June.

Kean, J. M., and Personke, C. 1976. The Language Arts, Teaching and Learning in the Elementary School. St. Martin's Press, Inc., New York.

Loban, W. 1976. Language Development Kindergarten Through Grade Twelve, Number 18. National Council of Teachers of English. Urbana, Illinois.

Miller, J. F. (ed.) 1974. *A Developmental Approach Toward Assessing Communication Behavior in Children.* Waisman Center on Mental Retardation and Human Development. University of Wisconsin, Madison.

Miller, Jon F. 1981. Assessing Language Production in Children. University Park Press, Baltimore.

Nelson, L. 1976. Language Development Outline. Department of Communicative Disorders, University of Wisconsin, Madison. (unpublished)

Olswang, L., Kriegsman, E., and Mastergeorge, A. 1982. Facilitating functional requesting in pragmatically impaired children. Language, speech and hearing services in schools. Asha, October. 13:202–217.

Paramore, B., and D'Amelio, D., 1982. Social Studies. Scott Foresman and Co., Glenview, IL.

Quigley, C. N. 1972. We Live in Communities. Ginn Publishing Co., Columbus, OH.

Sanders, E. R. 1972. When are speech sounds learned? J. Speech Hear. Disord. 37:55–63.

Speas, J., Ochoa, A., Cherryholmes, C., and Manson, G. 1979. Studying Cultures, T. E. (Grade 4). McGraw-Hill Book Co., New York.

Stark, J. 1981. Reading: What needs to be assessed? Top. Lang. Disord. 1:87–94.

Suppes, P., and Suppes, J. 1968. Sets and numbers: K. Singer mathematics program. Singer Company, New York.

Templin, M. 1957. Certain Language Skills in Children. University of Minnesota, Minneapolis.

Tough, J. 1977a. Listening to Children Talking. Drake Educational Associates, Great Britain.

Tough, J. 1977b. The Development of Meaning. John Wiley and Sons, Inc., New York.

Wellman, B., Case, I., and Mengert, I. 1931. Speech sounds of young children. Child Welf. 5:1–82.

Yoder, D. E., and Miller, J. F. 1972. A syntax teaching program. In: J. E. McLean, D. E. Yoder and R. L. Schiefelbusch (eds.), Language Intervention with the Retarded. University Park Press, Baltimore.

Suggested Readings

Berlin, Laura J., Blank, M., and Rose, S. A. 1980. The language of instruction: The hidden complexities. Top. Lang. Disord. December, 1:1.

Berry, M. 1980. Teaching Linguistically Handicapped Children. Prentice-Hall, Inc., Englewood Cliffs, NJ.

Binder, M. J. 1976. People and Change. Silver Burdett Co., Morristown, NJ.

Bloom, L. 1978. *Readings in Language Development.* John Wiley and Sons, Inc., New York.
This series of readings in language development provides an excellent overview on the description of children's language, the acquisition of use, content and form, and the interaction between comprehension and production.

Calfee, R. (ed.). 1982. Assessment of formal school language: Reading, writing and speaking. Top. Lang. Disord., September. 2.

Cazden, C. B. 1972. Child Language and Education. Holt, Rinehart and Winston, Inc., New York.

Loban, W. 1976. Language Development: Kindergarten through Grade Twelve. National Council of Teachers of English, Urbana, Illinois.

This monograph is a continuation of a series of research reports sponsored by the National Council of Teachers of English. It follows 211 children from kindergarten through grade 12 and is concerned with the structure of children's language at the various stages of development.

Lucas, E. V. 1980. Semantic and Pragmatic Language Disorders. Aspen Systems Corp., Germantown, MD.

Miller, J., Yoder, D., and Schiefelbusch, R. (eds.). 1983. Contemporary Issues in Language Intervention. Asha Reports, MD.

Polloway, E., and Smith Jr., J. 1982. Teaching Language Skills to Exceptional Learners. Love Publishing Co., Denver.

Tough, J. 1976. Listening to Children Talking. Ward Lock Educational, London.
This excellent manual is a guide to the appraisal of children's use of language. It focuses on the function (pragmatics) of language in various situations. The book provides assessment and intervention strategies.

Wiig, E. H., and Semel, E. M. 1976. Language Disabilities in Children and Adolescents. Charles E. Merrill Publishing Co., Columbus, OH.
This book provides a framework for regular and special educators to analyze language deficits and developing strategies to remediate these deficits. The underlying principle put forth in this book is that deficits in language and the areas of language underlie problems in reading and other learning disabilities.

Withrow, F. B., and Nygren, C. J. 1976. Language Materials and Curriculum Management for The Handicapped Learner. Charles E. Merrill Publishing Co., OH.

Part *Three*
Implementing the Process

Although Parts I and II describe and elaborate the process of the interaction of language in academics, Part III is the "proof of the pudding"—the ability of the reader to use this process in analyzing difficulties in academic subjects.

Academic Subjects— Implementation

Three subject areas (mathematics, social studies, and science) were selected to demonstrate the process.

In mathematics, examples are divided into primary and intermediate elementary levels. The primary math lesson includes sets and borrowing; the intermediate elementary lessons include place value and fractions. These particular content areas were chosen because of the difficulties experienced by both students and teachers that were observed from *the authors' observations* in the classroom. These observations reflected the concern expressed in the literature about the same difficulties.

The lessons selected for social studies and science represent further examples of reading in the content area. The examples in math, social studies, and science serve as models to illustrate the problems of language comprehension and use in reading in the content areas. Any other subject areas could serve this function as well.

Limitations

The analysis of language interaction provides basic information about the effect of language on a student's academic performance. It is *impor-* *tant* for the reader to realize that other variables, such as the decoding, computation, and writing skills of the student are equally important to assess. However, obtaining comprehensive information for successful intervention requires the inclusion of language analysis. Not including the language analysis could result in the current complaint of education that students have *difficulty in applying their basic skills to solve problems.*

Procedures for Analyzing Examples

A summary form of language interaction analysis is provided for each example. In some examples, the form is completed in its entirety and the formulation of hypotheses and implications for instruction are provided. In other examples, the summary analyses forms are partially completed or blank so that the reader is given the opportunity to gain experience in completing the analysis.

In situations where the information obtained on the summary analysis form is not sufficient enough to formulate hypotheses, the teacher is then advised to use the analysis form provided for each component of the triad (see Chapters 4, 5, and 6) for more detailed information.

Chapter 7
Mathematics

Sets
Subtraction
Place Value
Fractions
Decimals

I hear, and I forget
I see, and I remember
I do, and I understand

Chinese Proverb

Math encompasses more than the factual operations of addition, subtraction, multiplication, and division; more than any other academic subject, it requires a basic language and conceptual repertoire as prerequisites for the development of abstractions that are necessary for problem solving. These language and conceptual demands are evident in early mathematic tasks. Consider what is involved in the objectives of an instructional task in first grade (Thoburn, 1982a, p. 1).

Objectives
1.1 Display *understanding* of numbers and numerals 0–10 (comprehension)
1.2 Show the *order* of numbers 0–10 (seriation)
1.3 Identify which of two numbers is *greater/less* (comparatives)
1.4 Solve problems involving *comparison* of numbers (comparatives/critical thinking)
1.5 Display *understanding* of ordinals first–seventh (comprehension/seriation)

The following concept words (vocabulary) were used in these objectives:

greater	one	six	first	sixth
less	two	seven	second	seventh
number	three	eight	third	
numeral	four	nine	fourth	
zero	five	ten	fifth	

Objective 1.4 requires critical thinking at an elementary level in order to solve the problems. One of the goals in math is to teach logical think-ing to solve problems. Yet, math operations are often taught and learned in a rote manner. This is not to imply that rote learning of operations is undesirable. However, a problem in rote learning may occur if the student does not acquire the understanding and use of the concepts and language underlying the rote operations. According to Carpenter et al. (1981):

> One of the consequences of students learning mathematical skills by rote is that they cannot apply the skills they have learned to solve problems. In general, NAEP results showed that the majority of students at all age levels had difficulty with any nonroutine problem that required some analysis or thinking. *It appears that students have not learned basic problem-solving skills* (p. 146).

This is exemplified in the following example (Skypek, 1981):

> A graduate student, investigating "meaningful mathematics learning" showed this card
>
> $$7 \times 5$$
>
> to Kenneth, a sixth grader in a highly selective private school, and asked, "What does this mean to you?" "35." "Good. Can you tell me what it means?" "Oh, you want a story." He hummed for a few seconds and then announced, "That's hard." Finally, he said, "Well, it's like you have seven apples and five apples and you decide to multiply them instead of add them." When asked how he knew *when* to multiply, he responded, "When I see the times sign." Kenneth volunteered to do some "hard" multiplication and was flawless in processing 365×87. Kenneth had learned well his paper-and-pencil computations, but the mechanistic procedures seemed devoid of meaning (p. 13).

The research of another mathematics educator (Zweng, 1979), who listened to students in third, fourth, fifth, and sixth grades solve over 2,400 story problems, indicated that one fact was clear:

Children have almost no language with which to communicate about solving problems (p. 2).

The authors' observaton of classroom activities support Zweng's point of view. On the other hand, however, the students may not have the opportunity to express or develop the language. Through teacher questions and the modeling of language use, the students will learn to expand their language. Knight and Hargis (1977) provided three major entities showing how vital language is to *reading* in math:

1. *The grammar* of one-to-one correspondence would include the concept of *how many* and the vocabulary of *every, each, each one of, one of.*
2. *The noun phrase* would include *one of the blocks, a block, some blocks, an apple.*
   The articles *a, an,* specify oneness, whereas the article *some* denotes value greater than one.
3. The syntax of comparative construction most often is seen in story problems. For example:
   Bill ran a mile in six minutes.
   Jane ran *as fast as* Bill.
   How fast did Jane run?
   To solve this problem, the student must understand the comparative construction of *as fast as* which implies equality. Understanding that syntax of comparative constructions appears to be essential for solving math problems (p. 425).

If the student has difficulty with the above language entities in reading math, he or she will experience similar difficulty in writing math. Writing math involves an understanding of oral and written language, sentence structure, and vocabulary. In addition, higher math requires the transfer of these linguistic abilities to a new symbolic form. Solving a math problem requires a logical argument constructed in a similar fashion to that of a paragraph. A math problem used in an eighth grade class illustrates this construction (Skypek, 1981, p. 13):

$V = \frac{1}{3} \times B \times h$ (simple sentence)

If $B = 18$ and $h = 8$,   (complex sentence,
then $V = \frac{1}{3} \times 18 \times 8$. cause and effect, if/then)

Thus, $V = 48$.   (simple sentence)

In paragraph form, the problem would be stated as follows:

> V equals one-third times B times h. If B equals 18 and h equals 8, then V equals one-third times 18 times 8. Thus, V equals 48.

The inability of students to use language, either in oral or written form in order to explain how the problem is solved is a contributing factor to the experiences of math failure.

In summary, Skypek (1981) emphasized that:

Mathematics teaching and learning experiences should be symbolized in the verbal codes of ordinary language at both the oral and written levels before superimposing the coding scheme of language notations (p. 15).

This point of view reinforces the contention of the authors that language cannot be taught in a vacuum. It must be taught within all academic content areas.

Sets

Curriculum materials at the kindergarten level use paper-and-pencil tasks to teach the concepts of *sets, equality,* and *difference.* Many first- and second-grade teachers may assume that students have basic concepts for starting math because of kindergarten-level experiences in sorting, classifying, ordering, etc. Several questions may be raised regarding this assumption:

1. Have the experiences of sorting shapes or colors been related to relevant experiences?

2. Has sufficient experience been provided to develop these and other concepts from concrete to abstract, and from social uses to the math task?

3. Does the student understand the concept (receptive)? Is he able to use the concept in the performance of a math task (expressive)?

4. Is the student performing only in a rote-learning fashion?

These questions should be kept in mind for the following example on sets. They should be of assistance in analyzing whether students have the prerequisite concepts of one-to-one correspondence, sorting, classifying with one or more attributes, conservation of number, and seriation.

Demonstration Example A

The following example is derived from part of a videotape of a lesson on sets with two students, 6 years of age.

Teacher: Okay, now let's look at equal sets.

Displays card

What does this say? (Points to equal sign)

Student: Set is equal to set.

Teacher: Good. I am going to make a set here.

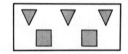 red squares
blue triangles

Robert, would you make an equal set for me there?

Robert: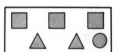
one green square
two blue squares
two green triangles
one blue circle

Teacher: Robert, are you making it equal? Are the two sets equal?
Greg, are these two sets equal?

(Do Robert and Greg have the concept of equal?)

Greg: No.

Teacher: Why not?

Greg: Because they're not the same.

Teacher: Let's see if Greg can do it. (Sets up another example)

(Greg completes the task correctly.)

Teacher: Are they equal now? Robert, are they equal?

Robert: (Counts) 1–2–3–4.

Teacher: How are they equal?

Robert: Because they are four.

Teacher: They both have four. And Greg, how did you make them equal?

Greg: Same size.

(Is Greg trying to match teacher's set visually?)

Teacher: Very good. Let's try this again. Ready?

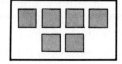 four green squares
two red squares

Robert: They are all squares.

Teacher: You are right. Robert, can you make a set equal to this one?

Robert: 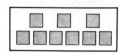 six green squares
three red squares

Teacher: Robert, are those two sets equal? Are they? Why are they?

(Teacher's questions are confusing. Teacher asks three questions in a row, without pausing.)

Robert: They are red and green.

Teacher: They are both red and green. Is that how they are equal? There are red ones and there are green ones there, and they are all what?

Greg: All the same.

Teacher: Why are they equal?

Greg: They are the same size.

Teacher: Robert, you said they were the same color; Greg, you said they were the same size. Now what do we need? They have to be the same . . . ?

Robert: Shape.

Teacher: Very good. How many reds do you have?

Robert: (Counts) 1–2–3.

Teacher: And now what? Now are they equal? How many reds do I have in my set?

Robert: (Counts) 1–2. (Removes 1 red from his set.)

Teacher: How many greens do the sets have?

Greg: 4.

Teacher: And how many reds?

Greg: 2.

Teacher: So, they're the same what?

Greg: Amount.

Teacher: The same amount and the same number, so this set is equal to this set.

Figure 7.1 shows the analysis of the language interaction in this lesson.

Implications for Instruction A set is defined as "a collection of any kind of things belonging together" (Williams and Shuard, 1970, p. 30). Sets can be put together, combined into a whole, as well as separated into parts. This operation is a precursor to *addition, subtraction,* and *comparison* and involves sequencing as well as the important language concepts of *all, some, more, less, enough, next to, before,* and *after.*

Figure 7.1 *Analysis of Language Interaction—Sets/Matching*

Identification
Name:
Age: 6

Instructional
level:
First grade
Date:

Subject:
Math
Objective:
Equal sets

Specific
task:
Matching

I. Language content/concepts

A.   *Explicit (vocabulary)*   B.   *Implicit (concepts/operations)*

equal	number	four	**1.**	Classification		**2.** Conservation	
sets	size	two		Sorting	**X**	**3.** Time	
red	shape	same		Class inclusion	__	**4.** Seriation	**X**
green	blue			Class exclusion	__	**5.** Space	
blue	amount			Regrouping	__	**6.** Causality	__

Comments: _____

II.

Teacher/instructional language (written or oral)

A.   Explanation/direction: Simple **X** Complex __ Confusing ____

B.   Use of multiple concepts: _____

C.   Questions: Form   __**what, how, why**__   Type   __**narrow**__

D.   Speaking mode: Length _____ Rate _____

Comments: _____

III.   Student language (What requisites does the student need?)

A.   Comprehension

Vocabulary: __**equal, sets, color, number**__

Syntax (sentence structure):   __**simple sentences; question form**__

B.   Production

Speaking: __**none—demonstrates through manipulation**__

Reading: _____

Writing: _____

Comments: _____

IV.   Hypotheses: 1.   The students may not have understood the teacher's expectations. (objectives: equality or equivalency?)

2.   The students may not have had the prerequisite concepts/operations for the task. (sorting, classification)

3.   The students may not have understood the question forms "how" and "why."

Teaching the student to *sort, combine,* and *order* on a particular dimension or property involves considerable teacher direction. The teacher must be acutely aware of the directions given to the student. This means that he or she must understand the responses required by the task and not complicate the direction with other verbalizations, which may confuse the student.

All of the concerns expressed in the hypotheses may have been operating in the specific task. Teachers cannot test out and develop teaching strategies for all of the hypotheses simultaneously. It will be more profitable to start with what may be the most crucial hypothesis in the task—in this case, Hypothesis 2. The teacher's knowledge of the student will be a factor in determining the priorities of the hypotheses.

Hypothesis 2   The students may not have had the prerequisite concepts/operations for the task: sorting and classification.

Intervention strategies were constructed to find out whether the students understood the concepts/operations necessary for the task. Blocks of different colors, sizes, and shapes were set in front of the students. The teacher requested each student to give her the following blocks:

All those of a single color (first, yellow; second, blue; third, red)
  All responses from the students were correct.

All those that were round
  Greg sorted correctly.
  Robert sorted incorrectly; gave the teacher all orange blocks of different shapes.

All those that were square
  Greg responded correctly.
  Robert responded incorrectly.

All the square blue ones
  Greg responded correctly.
  Robert responded incorrectly.

The following exchange took place:

Teacher: Robert, why did you give me these? (The teacher points to his arrangement of the last exercise)
Robert: Because they are blue/real blue/dark blue.

Analysis of the responses revealed that:

1. Greg could sort by single as well as multiple attributes of color, shape, and size.

2. Robert could only sort by one attribute—that of color.

Further testing also revealed that neither student could classify (that is, make a pile of blocks based on a common characteristic) let alone explain why they had constructed the piles as they did.

Problems of students' readiness for a task such as the one illustrated may form the basis for failure in learning later math tasks. If Robert does not learn how to sort on single and multiple attributes and to classify, he can be expected to have difficulty with addition and subtraction (class inclusion). Further hypotheses-testing will be necessary to determine whether Robert understands seriation as well as one-to-one corre-

spondence. Strategies for testing these hypotheses may be obtained from Lavatelli (1973b) and Williams and Shuard (1970), and Copeland (1974).

The teacher's language is also an important variable in this task. *Hypothesis 1* indicates that the students may not have understood the teacher's expectations. Sometimes the teacher's expectation is not made clear by the type and form of the questions used. Thus, the student may not be able to respond appropriately. The implication then is that the student has failed when in fact it was the teacher's inappropriate question or direction that caused the failure. The teacher must plan precisely what information he or she is expecting from the student and then plan the type and form of questions to be used.

The experiences of sorting and classifying can help to expand student language as well as concepts/operations so that the student can use the language of math to solve problems such as the following:

1.
$$
\boxed{\begin{smallmatrix} \bullet\ \bullet\ \bullet \\ \bullet\ \bullet \end{smallmatrix}} = \boxed{5}
$$

$$= \left\{ \begin{array}{l} \textit{Implicit} \\ \text{1:1 correspondence} \\ \text{equality} \end{array} \right\}$$

2. $27 = 2 \text{ tens } \boxed{} \text{ ones}$

$$\left\{ \begin{array}{l} \textit{Implicit} \\ \text{equality} \\ \text{regrouping} \end{array} \right\}$$

3. ☐☐☐☐☐☐☐

  a. Think about taking this subset away. (Answer: $7 - 3 = 4$)

$$\left\{ \begin{array}{l} \textit{Explicit} \\ \text{equality} \\ \text{class inclusion} \\ \text{grouping} \\ \text{difference} \\ \text{subtract, take away} \\ \text{math symbols} \\ \quad \text{used in answer} \end{array} \right\}$$

  b. Write a subtraction sentence.
  c. When we subtract 3 from 7, the difference is 4.

Subtraction/Borrowing

"To borrow" in a math task means to change or take from one group to another. This involves skills in grouping and regrouping as well as understanding the vocabulary.

Implicit in regrouping are skills of sorting, classification, conservation, and one-to-one correspondence. These concepts and operations form the basis for math and must be mastered at the early elementary grade levels. Otherwise, the student will experience difficulty in later math tasks, such as subtraction/borrowing.

This is illustrated in the following problems, presented to a student, 10 years of age, who is repeating fourth grade.

Demonstration Example B

Teacher: I am going to write a problem on the paper and I want you to tell me what kind of problem it is. What kind of problem is it?

$$
\begin{array}{r}
66 \\
- \ 6 \\
\hline
\end{array}
$$

Student: Take-away problem.
Teacher: You are really thinking hard. Read the problem.
Student: 66 take away 6.
Teacher: That's right. What are you going to do first?
Student: Add one column.

(*Does student understand the math signs + and − ?*)

Teacher: Let's take a look at that again. What kind of problem is it?
Student: Subtraction.

(*There is a 50% chance of the correct response. If not addition, then the answer must be subtraction.*)

Teacher: It is a subtraction problem. So what do you have to do first?
Student: Take away 6.
Teacher: What does it say in the ones column?
Student: 66 take away 6.
Teacher: Well, what's the question you have to ask about that? Can I do it?

Demonstration Example C

Teacher: What does this problem say?

$$
\begin{array}{r}
50 \\
- 38 \\
\hline
\end{array}
$$

Student: 50 take away 38.
Teacher: Okay, what are you going to do?
Student: Take away.
Teacher: Okay, it is a subtraction problem. What part of the problem do we have to do first?
Student: Ones.
Teacher: Okay, what does it say in the ones column?
Student: 0 take away 8.
Teacher: Okay, 0 take away 8. Can I do that?
Student: Yes . . . no.
Teacher: Show me 0 sticks.
Student: I can't.
Teacher: Why can't you show me 0 sticks?
Student: Cuz it says on the paper.
Teacher: What does it say?
Student: 0 take away.
Teacher: Okay, it means we have 0 to begin with. How many is 0?
Student: None.
Teacher: Right, so if I don't have any, can I take 8 away?
Student: No.
Teacher: Okay, what do I have to do?
Student: Borrow.
Teacher: Finish the problem now.
Student:
$$
\begin{array}{r}
50 \\
- 38 \\
\hline
28 \\
\end{array}
$$

The teacher began to question whether the student understood the operation of borrowing or whether he was confused about the 0. Therefore, she put another set of problems on the blackboard.

Demonstration Example D

22	40	20	56	32	34
−10	− 5	+34	−46	−30	+30

R's answers:

11		11		21	
2̸2̸	40	2̸0̸	56	3̸2̸	34
−10	− 5	+34	−46	−30	+30
02	41	46	10	02	64

The student's answers indicated inconsistency when he was asked to respond to the + and − math signs and also when asked to borrow. The Analysis of Language Interaction form in Figure

Figure 7.2 *Analysis of Language Interaction—Subtraction/Borrowing*

Identification	*I.* *Language content/concepts*
Name:	*A.* *Explicit (vocabulary)* *B.* *Implicit (concepts/operations)*
Age: 10	

I. *Language content/concepts*

A. *Explicit (vocabulary)*

take away	ones
first	zero
subtraction	add
plus/minus	
_____	
_____	

B. *Implicit (concepts/operations)*

1.	Classification	*2.* Conservation	X
	Sorting	_ *3.* Time	_
	Class inclusion	X *4.* Seriation	_
	Class exclusion	X *5.* Space	_
	Regrouping	_ *6.* Causality	_

Comments: _____

Subject:
Math

II. *Teacher/instructional language (written or oral)*

Objective:
Subtraction

A. Explanation/direction: Simple **X** Complex_ Confusing____

B. Use of multiple concepts: _____

C. Questions: Form   what, why, how, "can Type   narrow____
                                              I do it"

D. Speaking mode: Length _____ Rate _____
Comments:_____

III. *Student language (What requisites does the student need?)*

A. Comprehension

**Specific
task:**

Vocabulary: explicit vocabulary dealing with concept of
                 subtraction

Syntax (sentence structure): Teacher's questions

Borrowing

B. Production

Speaking: numbers only
Reading: numbers only
Writing: numbers only

Comments: _____

IV. *Hypotheses:* **1.** Does the student have the operation prerequisites for
                       subtraction-borrowing: class inclusion, exclusion and
                       conservation?

2. The student may be confused by the math signs $(+, -)$.

3. The teacher's language (questions) may not have guided
        the student in solving the problem.

4. The student may not understand the concept of zero in
        subtraction.

7.2 permits the formulation of hypotheses toward trying to solve the student's difficulties.

Implications for Instruction This particular observation was selected because of the many problems that can account for the student's difficulty in subtraction. The source of these problems is the lack of the cognitive and linguistic skills necessary for the operation of subtraction/borrowing. To subtract/borrow requires skills in class inclusion, regrouping, and conservation. Before a student is able to subtract, he or she must be able to add, i.e., apply class inclusion before doing class exclusion and to group before he can regroup. In addition, the student must master the signs for these operations. For illustrative purposes, only the following hypotheses have been selected to be analyzed.

Hypothesis 1   Did the student have the operation prerequisites for subtraction/borrowing: class inclusion, exclusion, and conservation?

The teacher first determined whether the student could group (class inclusion) by giving him single-column as well as double-column addition problems. The student solved these problems correctly.

Demonstration Example E

4	0	3	7	34	23	10
+0	+2	+1	+1	+30	+14	+33
4	2	4	8	64	37	43

Next, the teacher tested to see whether the student could subtract where borrowing was not required (class exclusion).

6	8	4	5	56	34
−2	−6	−4	−0	−46	−30
4	2	0	0	10	04

Analysis   With the exception of 5 − 0, the student completed these problems correctly. The error for the incorrect answer may have been attributable to carelessness, but it cannot be overlooked. When addition and subtraction problems were presented in Problem D, the student exhibited confusion in deciding whether to add or subtract. Whether this is because of difficulties in understanding class inclusion and exclusion and the application of the symbols + and − to these operations will need additional assessment by the teacher.

Further analysis of Example D reveals great confusion about borrowing. The student understood the mechanics of borrowing i.e. taking from one group to change another, but the *concept of borrowing* and *when to borrow* confused him. The teacher will have to determine if the student can:

1. Group (class inclusion, concept of *all*)

2. Regroup (class exclusion, concept of *some*)

3. Conserve (rearrange *parts* of a group while the *whole* remains the same)

4. Do the three operations listed in a concrete manner before applying the operation of subtraction/borrowing to a more abstract form—paper-and-pencil activity.

The *crucial* point here is the transition from the concept/operation learned in a concrete manipulative manner to the numeral in a paper-and-pencil activity.

Hypothesis 4   The student may not understand the concept of 0 in subtraction.

Zero has an identity of its own just as 1, 4, 5, etc. The *number* which represents the empty set is 0. For example, a student may have one penny, two marbles and 0 pencils. Just as numbers are taught to represent a class of objects or things, so the 0 must be taught to represent a class of empty sets (Russell, 1956).

According to Williams and Shuard (1970):

> It is important for the later development of a number system that students should come to think of 0 as a number rather than as a symbol for the absence of numbers. The use of numbers in measuring, where 0 symbolizes the starting point of the ruler, and in graphical work, may help to set 0 among the other numbers and so, in particular, to smooth the introduction of positive and negative directed numbers at a later stage (p. 64).

It is difficult for students to transfer a task from the concrete to the abstract. What may be thought of as concrete, such as worksheets in a math workbook, may indeed be very abstract to the student. This especially is true when manipulative devices are provided to help the student learn a math operation and then the student is expected to transfer the operation immediately to a workbook page. The transition to paper-and-pencil tasks may be made too soon.

Instead, intervention strategies with such students could include the following objectives:

1. Determine whether the student can consistently count correctly with manipulative devices, such as sticks, pencils, etc. The question is, does he have one-to-one correspondence?

2. If the student does not demonstrate consistent performance in one-to-one correspondence, the teacher may have to test whether the concepts of conservation of number, seriation, and classification are

well-established. For more information concerning these tasks, refer to Copeland, (1974); Lavatelli (1973a); and Lorton (1972).

3. If the student demonstrates adequate performance in the concept areas of conservation of number, seriation, and classification, then using manipulative devices, proceed to duplicating the workbook task.

4. The teacher may have to pair the manipulative devices with the numeral itself. Fade out the manipulative devices and present numeral only.

5. Use workbook pages only.

Place Value

Classroom observations and concerns expressed in the literature indicate that place value is an area of difficulty for many students. According to Carpenter et al. (1981):

> Most 9-year-olds were less successful in tasks that directly involved place value notions (p. 12).

It is not surprising that students have difficulty with place value when it is introduced at the second- or third-grade level because of the conceptual and linguistic requirements. Some of the possible sources of this difficulty in a third-grade textbook (MacMillan, 1976) are:

1. *Teacher curricular expectations*
   a. Students must *count* and *group* objects by 10
   b. Students must learn that:
      meaning of digit depends on the value of the place it occupies in a numeral as well as on the digit itself (p. 28)
   c. Students must know *order* of numbers
   d. Students must show *relationship* of 1, 10, 100, 1,000s
   e. Students must use *ordinals* to describe position

2. *Concepts inherent in place value*
   a. Classification (grouping, regrouping)
   b. Seriation (order, comparative)
   c. Conservation (reversibility)

3. *Student language prerequisites*
   a. Students must be able to transfer from saying the number (4,079) to reading the number (the value of a digit) to writing the number (4,079) from an oral direction
   b. Students must comprehend and use the following concept words (vocabulary):

numeral	ones	order	least
number	place	greater	nearest
digit	hundred	less	round
tens	thousands	greatest	nearer
more	less		

   c. Students must be able to transfer concept vocabulary to math shorthand

thousands	$\diagdown\diagup$
hundreds	$\diagup$
tens	| | | | |
ones	••••

Observations of classroom lessons illustrate some of the foregoing points. Each demonstration will be analyzed and followed by implications for instruction.

Demonstration Example F

Teacher: Do you remember yesterday's lesson? In math there is a magic number. Do you know what it is?

Students: 9, 7, 6, 9, 100, 11.

Teacher: I like to think of 10 as a magic number. Do you have any idea why?

First student: 10 takes all the numbers in (recites by 10s)

Second student: It's like when you have 10, you add 8, it's 18; 9, it's 19.

Teacher: You have 10 toes, 10 fingers, 10 ones is 1 ten. If I put 10 tens together, what would I have?

Students: 100

Teacher: Read this number (The teacher points to number on place value chart) 622.

Student: Six hundred and twenty-two.

Teacher: Read this number.

Student: Two thousand and two.

Teacher: (Writes 4,892.) What does this say?

Student: Four thousand and eighty-nine.

Teacher: Now do it this way. (The teacher cups her hands around the 4)

Student: Four thousand.
Teacher: (Cups hand around 892.)
Student: Eight hundred and ninety-two.
Teacher: Who can tell us the value of the digit 1 underlined in 6$\underline{1}$6,000?
Student: Sixteen thousand.
Teacher: (Writes 493,546.) What is the value of 9?
Student: Nine thousand.
Teacher: No, Ninety thousand.

Figure 7.3 shows the analysis of language interaction for this lesson.

Implications for Instruction The ramifications of place value permeate all of the basic operations of math, such as addition, subtraction, multiplication, and division. For instance, consider the implication of place value in students' difficulty with four- and five-digit numbers.

Hypotheses 2 and 3 seem to have the highest priority for intervention.

Hypothesis 2 Can the student group and regroup by tens to form hundreds and thousands?

Regrouping by tens is an operation in classification. It requires that the student be able to combine parts (ones) to form whole (tens) and recognize the equality. Regroupings may be simple for the student to understand because so many demonstrations can be done easily through manipulative materials at a concrete level. However, when the task is expanded to increase the place values, then the task of regrouping becomes more complex and abstract. For example, ten 10s equal 100; ten 100s equal 1,000; ten 1,000s equal 10,000, etc.

Students usually learn this progression in regrouping in a rote fashion. What they may not understand is the additive value of the tens and the abstract math language used to symbolize these groupings, i.e., periods and commas as well as the math sentence itself, such as 10 100s = 1,000. Included in the notion of additive value is the operation of seriation. Recall that the students' ability to talk about seriation requires the comprehension of comparatives (*greater, greatest, more than, less than,* etc.) and ordinal numbers.

Instructional language usually refers to the grouping of ones into tens as *renaming tens.*

Teachers must be aware that usage of the term *renaming* may obscure the important operation of grouping and regrouping, and thus, they may overlook whether the students have the basic prerequisites of classification for this task.

It is necessary for the teacher to develop another perspective of looking at students' difficulties in specific instructional tasks.

Hypothesis 3 Is the student able to read the digits *left to right,* giving each digit its proper place value? Is the student able to group the digit by periods from *right to left*? (seriation and reversibility)

Copeland (1974) suggested that the ability to read digits left to right and right to left requires reversibility of thought and an understanding of the qualitative relationship that exists between the numbers (seriation). In Example F, one student was unable to read the digits left to right when he read 2,020 as 2,002. Another student grouped (right to left) and read the value of the digit $\underline{1}$ in 6$\underline{1}$6,000 as 16,000.

Analysis By third grade, the student should be able to reverse his or her thought and do regrouping. They may have the mental operation of reversibility but might be unable to use and apply it in a variety of academic tasks. This may be attributable to a lack of instructional direction in demonstrating the relationship of reversibility in reading, math, science, etc.

Additional implications for instruction follow Demonstration Example G.

Demonstration Example G (Fourth-Fifth Grades, Low Group)—Place Value[1]

Teacher: We will do a little review today. (Puts number 458,327,901 on board.) How many digits are in the numeral?
Student: Nine.
Teacher: You can group them by three and separate each set of three by a comma. You can tell the periods by the commas. Each group of three is called a what?
Student: Period.

---

[1] Adapted from Macmillan, 1976.

Figure 7.3 *Analysis of Language Interaction—Place Value/Reading Periods*

Identification	**I.** *Language content/concepts*
Name:	A. *Explicit (vocabulary)* B. *Implicit (concepts/operations)*
Age: 8–9	

I.   *Language content/concepts*

A.   *Explicit (vocabulary)*

tens   digit

ones   value

hundreds magic number

thousands

_____

Comments: _____

B.   *Implicit (concepts/operations)*

1. Classification		**2.** Conservation	X
Sorting		**3.** Time	__
Class inclusion	X	**4.** Seriation	X
Class exclusion	__	**5.** Space	__
Regrouping	X	**6.** Causality	__

Identification

Name:

Age: 8–9

Instructional level:

3rd grade

Date:

Subject:

Math

Objective:

Place value

Specific task:

Reading periods

II.   *Teacher/instructional language (written or oral)*

A.   Explanation/direction: Simple _X_ Complex__   Confusing _X_

B.   Use of multiple concepts: _____

C.   Questions: Form   ____who, what____   Type   ___narrow___

D.   Speaking mode: Length   _____ok_____ Rate _____

Comments:_____

III.   *Student language (What requisites does the student need?)*

A.   Comprehension

Vocabulary: tens, ones, hundred, thousands, digit, value number

Syntax (sentence structure):   question forms

B.   Production

Speaking: ____numerals and periods_____

Reading: ____numerals and periods_____

Writing: _____

Comments: _____

IV.   Hypotheses: 1.   Does the teacher's use of the term "magic number" interfere with the student's comprehension of grouping by tens?

2.   Can the student group and regroup by tens to form hundreds and thousands?

3.   (a) Is the student able to read the digits left to right giving each digit its proper place value?

(b) Is the student able to group the digits by periods from right to left?

Teacher: That's just another word for group. (Teacher draws following chart on board and points to it):

Periods								
Millions			Thousands			Ones		
100	10	1	100	10	1	100	10	1
	458			327			901	

Teacher: You remember the pattern that keeps repeating here?

Student: Yes—ones, 10s, 100s.

Teacher: I'm going to say a number and you're going to have to write it. I may add 0s at the beginning, middle, or end. If I add a 0 before, does it change the number?

Student: No.

Teacher: Zero after 28 (writes 28, then puts in a 0).

Student: Two hundred and eighty.

Teacher: How do I write four thousand and five? You tell me digit by digit what to write.

Student: Four - zero - five.

Teacher: I've got 405.

Student: Four - zero - zero - five.

Another student comments, "You forgot the comma."

Teacher: When you have 4, it's optional to use a comma.

(*This is a confusing remark.*)

Teacher: Five, you have to and from then on.

Teacher: What if I say twenty-six thousand, one hundred and twenty-eight? Someone tell me what to write. I'll give you a piece of paper so you can write the number and not forget it. Put down 26, 128, how you think it should be written.

Student: (Answers correctly.)

Teacher: Here's a hard one. How shall I write sixteen thousand and eleven?

First student: 160,11 (writes)

Second student: 16,0011 *(writes)*

Third student: 16,11 (writes)

Teacher: Each period is made up of how many numbers?

Student: Three.

Teacher: (Uses above answers to group by three. Uses chart to analyze place value.) How many ones?

Student: Eleven.

Teacher: One ten and one one.
Answer is sixteen thousand, no hundreds and eleven.
I said you have to have three places, not two or four.
When you write one, six, one, one, it isn't wrong. It's just that you don't know what place it is in.
What place is this in? ___16,001 (writes) (Points to place before 16.)

Student: Hundred thousand.

Teacher: We could say 016,001, but we said that if you put the 0 there, it doesn't mean anything. So actually, there are three places, but the 0 doesn't mean anything so we don't count it.

Teacher: Here's a new problem. When I write it out, I'll show you where the commas are. 47,286 (written on board). Commas are little hints. Let's see what answers you wrote on your paper.

Students: Answers: 470,286
47,1100
47,286

Teacher: Some people had 47,000,086. Were there any millions in the problem?

Figure 7.4 shows the analysis of language interaction for this lesson.

Implications for Instruction Although all of the hypotheses in this observation should be explored, Hypotheses 1 and 4 will be emphasized. (The implications in Hypotheses 2 and 3 are similar to those discussed in the previous example.)

Hypothesis 1 The teacher's use of language in explaining place value may have confused the student.

Figure 7.4 *Analysis of Language Interaction—Place Value/Reading and Writing Periods through Millions*

Identification
Name:
Age: 9–10
 	
Instructional level:
4–5 grade
Low
math group
Date:
 	
Subject:
Math
Objective:
Place value
 	
Specific task:
Reading and writing periods through millions
	I. Language content/concepts
	   A. Explicit (vocabulary) B. Implicit (concepts/operations)
	   <u>digits tens zero</u> **1.** Classification **2.** Conservation <u>X</u>
	   <u>numeral hundreds</u> Sorting <u>X</u> **3.** Time <u> </u>
	   <u>periods thousands</u> Class inclusion <u>X</u> **4.** Seriation <u>X</u>
	
	                Class exclusion **5.** Space
	   <u>comma millions</u> <u> </u> <u> </u>
	   <u>ones value</u> Regrouping <u>X</u> **6.** Causality <u> </u>
	   Comments: _____
	
	II. *Teacher/instructional language (written or oral)*
	   A. Explanation/direction: Simple <u>X</u> Complex__ Confusing <u>X</u>
	   B. Use of multiple concepts: _____
	   C. Questions: Form <u>**when, what**</u> Type <u>**narrow**</u>
	   D. Speaking mode: Length _____Rate _____
	   Comments: _____
	
	III. *Student language (What requisites does the student need?)*
	   A. Comprehension
	      Vocabulary: <u>**place value words**</u>
	      Syntax (sentence structure): <u>**question words**</u>
	   B. Production
	
	      Speaking: <u>**Must be able to say the numbers**</u>
	      Reading: <u>**Must be able to recognize the place value**</u>
	      Writing: <u>**Must be able to write the numbers in the correct order**</u>
	   Comments: _____
	
	IV. *Hypotheses:* **1.** The teacher's use of language in explaining place value may have confused the student.
	   2. Does the student have the concept of grouping and regrouping, conservation, and seriation?
	   3. Can the student apply the operation of reversibility in writing the numbers?
	   4. The students may have difficulty in writing the place value because they do not comprehend how the zero should be used.

Hypothesis 4 It is quite obvious that the teacher's language leaves much to be desired. In reviewing the teacher's statements, the reader will observe that the teacher's explanations and directions were lengthy and/or confusing. For example, in the direction, "You can group them by threes and separate each set of three by a comma; you can tell the periods by the commas," the students may experience confusion about the double meanings of the words *period* and *comma*. Both of these words are familiar to the student in reading and writing. Clear explanation and differentiation of the word period as a new name for group, and comma as a marker dividing the groups and subsets of a group must be made by the teacher if the student is to be successful in the task. In the direction, the teacher's explanation should have included pairing the new meaning of *period* with *group* so that the students could make the transition.

The students may have had difficulty in writing the place value because they did not comprehend how the 0 should be used.

In another instance the teacher might say,

"We could say 016,00 but we said that if you put 0s there, it doesn't mean anything. So actually there are three places, but the zero doesn't mean anything so we don't count it."

Here, the teacher language is not only confusing, but may also mislead the students' comprehension of the digit 0 in place value. Indeed, 0 is a digit and *has place value*. It does have meaning even if it does not have value, e.g. .012.

Students have difficulty with 0 in place value, particularly in the written form. The meaning of 0 changes, depending on its position in a numerical statement, e.g., .002, 2.02, and 200. Zeros should not be grouped by periods when first introduced into the lesson at this early stage of learning. After the students comprehend the meaning of the periods via the use of commas, then 0 should be introduced gradually, one period at a time. This allows the students to integrate the meaning and use of 0 into the acquisition of place value.

Fractions

Conservation of the whole is an essential condition for operational subdivision (Piaget et al., 1966, p. 311).

This is the essence of understanding fractions.

According to Copeland (1974), the concept of subdivision has a dual role: students must understand that the fraction is a part of the *original whole*; and also, the fraction is a *whole in itself*, which can continue to be subdivided. In addition to the operation of conservation of the whole or fractions, there are concepts such as order, space and temporality, depending on the context in which the fraction is used.

The vocabulary and concepts associated with fractions that are not well-developed by 9 years of age, according to the results of the Second National Assessment of Mathematics (Carpenter, et al., 1981), include *part, whole, greater than, less than, equivalent, denominator, numerator, proper, improper,* and *mixed.* In addition, the student is required to transpose oral and/or written words into a new written symbol system. This symbol system poses problems because of its abstract nature. Carpenter et al. (1981) illustrated this point:

1. Students may respond correctly to a teacher question by pointing to a *pictorial* representation of the fraction (comprehension).

2. The students may respond correctly to a multiple choice item by selecting the correct fractional numeral (comprehension).

3. They may have difficulty responding correctly when asked to express the correct fractional numeral (oral, pictorial, written) because this exercise requires them to *generate the response* (production)

An example from a textbook (Holt, 1978, grade 3) will help to clarify these points:

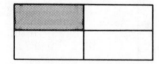

1. Look at this picture. How many parts are shown?

2. How many parts are shaded? Two, one, four?

3. Write a fractional numeral for $\frac{1}{4}$.

Carpenter's (1981) comments on fraction concepts showed that when children nine years of age were . . .

. . . required to *choose* or *write* the symbol representing the fraction when given the verbal description, about $\frac{7}{8}$ chose the correct symbol, but only a little over one-half wrote the correct symbol for the same fraction (p. 32).

This emphasizes the need for teachers to know that the kind of questions asked require different skills and modes of responding (comprehension/production).

Demonstration Example H (Third Grade)[2]

The objective of the following example is to compare fractional parts of a whole   Compare the following shaded and unshaded parts. Use the sign for *greater than* and *less than* (> <).

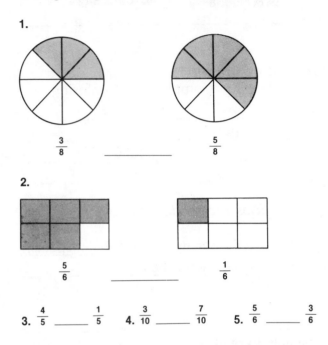

1.

$$\frac{3}{8} \underline{\hspace{2cm}} \frac{5}{8}$$

2.

$$\frac{5}{6} \underline{\hspace{2cm}} \frac{1}{6}$$

3. $\frac{4}{5}$ _____ $\frac{1}{5}$ **4.** $\frac{3}{10}$ _____ $\frac{7}{10}$ **5.** $\frac{5}{6}$ _____ $\frac{3}{6}$

Figure 7.5 shows an analysis of language interaction for this lesson.

Implications for Instruction   These hypotheses involve the concepts of the task and student language. Teacher language is implied in the instructional language in the task.

Hypothesis 1   Does the student understand the concept of whole and part? Two important operations are required—class inclusion and conservation. Class inclusion, an important skill in classification, is present in many math tasks, such as addition, subtraction, multiplication, division, place value, and fractions. It requires the comprehension and use of the words *all* and *some*, which are crucial to logical thinking. Copeland (1974) stated that:

> Not until a child is 9–10 years old is he usually able to use these words correctly in a logical sense for classification (p. 60).

_____

[2] Adapted from Nichols, E., Holt, 1978, p. 273.

All and *some* also relate to part/whole relationships. Fractions are a part (some) of the whole number (all).

In the discussion of the part/whole relationship in fractions, the operation of conservation must be considered. Regardless of how the whole is subdivided, it is always a part of the whole.

Analysis   Class inclusion and conservation have important considerations for intervention strategies. Intervention strategies that deal with the whole and parts at a concrete manipulative level may solve some of the problems in the comprehension of fractions, e.g., the cutting of a cake into parts to identify fractions. Unless these concrete experiences are provided, the students still may not understand that the whole may be divided in many ways as long as all parts are equal, i.e.:

$$\frac{3}{3} = 1; \frac{8}{8} = 1; \frac{16}{16} = 1$$

These concrete experiences should be related to the students' own experiences in daily living. For example, a school day (whole) can be divided in a variety of ways (parts) and displayed in a concrete visual representation (graph), stressing the fact that the school day is always 6 hours. This graph of a variety of experiences and the associated language will assist the student in transitioning to more abstract symbols used in writing fractions and their application to everyday affairs, including money, cooking, and time as well as academic subjects.

In addition to understanding the concept of fractions, the student may have difficulty deciding which operation to use in solving a word problem. The variables that may account for this failure are:

1. The student may not be able to do the operation.

2. The language of the word problem may contain information which is not presented sequentially or may be irrelevant.

3. The student may not have the math vocabulary, symbols, and/or sentence structure for verbalizing the concepts and method of computation in solving the problem.

Figure 7.5 Analysis of Language Interaction—Fractions/Comparing Fractional Parts

Identification

Name:

Age: 8–9

Instructional level:

Third grade

Date:

Subject:

Math

Objective:

Fractions

Specific task:

Comparing fractional parts

I. Language content/concepts
   A. Explicit (vocabulary)   B. Implicit (concepts/operations)
      greater than   1. Classification   2. Conservation X
      less than   Sorting   X 3. Time   __
      compare   Class inclusion   X 4. Seriation   X
      part   Class exclusion   __ 5. Space   X
      whole   Regrouping   __ 6. Causality   __
      Comments: _____

II. Teacher/instructional language (written or oral)
   A. Explanation/direction: Simple X   Complex __   Confusing ____
   B. Use of multiple concepts: none
   C. Questions: Form   none   Type _____
   D. Speaking mode: Length _____ Rate _____
      Comments: _____

III. Student language (What requisites does the student need?)
   A. Comprehension
      Vocabulary: comparative words (seriation); part/whole (spatial)
      Syntax (sentence structure):   simple sentences
   B. Production

      Speaking: _____
      Reading: ___ Must be able to read >   < _____
      Writing: ___ Must be able to write >   < _____
      Comments: _____

IV. Hypotheses: 1. Does the student understand the concept of whole and part (class inclusion and conservation)?

           2. Does the student comprehend and produce comparative words (seriation) (greater than, less than) and the symbolic representation (> <) of these words (seriation)?

Decimals

Difficulties with decimals parallel the difficulties with fractions (Payne, 1980). In both decimals and fractions, the student must be able to comprehend spatial representation (part/whole relationships). To ensure the development of spatial representation, verbal names (vocabulary) and sufficient concrete experiences must precede the use of symbolic math forms. Decimals are most commonly expressed in money.

Because money deals with part/whole relationships, fractions and percentages are also present. The notion of place value also underlies the use of decimals and percentages.

The analysis of student difficulties in money may be related to the concept of the part/whole relationship, the vocabulary used to represent these relationships, and the language context of the problem (sentence structure/syntax).

Practice Exercises

To give the reader the opportunity to practice the process of analyzing language interaction in math, several examples from textbooks are used. The reader should complete the analysis form provided for each example. The analysis must reflect: 1) the components of the triad present in the particular example; and 2) hypotheses formulated according to the instructions in Chapter 3.

Practice Exercise 1 (Third Grade)[3]

Objective To introduce the concept of n for logical thinking

Specific Task To name the whole numbers for n

1. Name the whole numbers that are correct answers for n. n is an even number less than 7 or $n = 9$. (0, 2, 4, 6, 9)

2. If $n < 3$, then $n = 2$,
   $n < 3$
   What does $n = $?

Practice Exercise 2[4]

Objective To provide experiences for writing fractions for parts of a set

Specific Task Written example

Write a fraction to describe each subset.

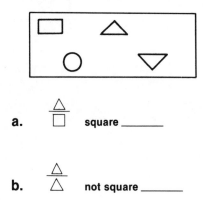

a. $\dfrac{\triangle}{\square}$ square _____

b. $\dfrac{\triangle}{\triangle}$ not square _____

Practice Exercise 3 (Third Grade)[5]

Objective To introduce calendar day, week, month, and year

Specific Task To develop equivalencies for day, week, month, and year

1. If December 3 is Thursday, what is the date of next Thursday? _____

2. If May 24 is Friday, what day of the week is May 31? _____

3. What day is 20 days from October 15? __

4. What day is 4 weeks from your birthday?

Practice Exercise 4 (Third Grade)[6]

Objective Place value

Specific Task Choose correct answer

What is the standard numeral for six hundred thousand, fifty seven?

1. 657
2. 6,057
3. 60,057
4. 600,057

Practice Exercise 5 (Third Grade)[7]

Objective Place value

Specific Task Counting by tens

Find the pattern. Copy and complete.
99,960, 99,970, _____ 100,000.

[3] Reprinted by permission from: Suppes, P. et al. (1976) The Random House Mathematics Program, Teacher's Ed., Grade 3, p. 148. Copyright © (1976) Random House, Inc.

[4] Reprinted by permission from: Suppes, P. et al. (1976) The Random House Mathematics Program, Teacher's Ed., Grade 3, p. 221. Copyright © (1976) Random House, Inc.

[5] Reprinted by permission from: Suppes, P. et al. (1976) The Random House Mathematics Program, Teacher's Ed., Grade 3, pp. 191–192. Copyright © (1976) Random House, Inc.

[6] Adapted from Nichols, E., 1978, p. 1.

[7] Adapted from Nichols, E., 1978, p. 33.

Identification

Name:

Age:

Instructional level:

Date:

Subject:

Objective:

Specific task:

I. *Language content/concepts*
   A.   *Explicit (vocabulary)*   B.   *Implicit (concepts/operations)*

   _____   **1.** Classification   **2.** Conservation __

   _____   Sorting __ **3.** Time __

   _____   Class inclusion __ **4.** Seriation __

   _____   Class exclusion __ **5.** Space __

   _____   Regrouping __ **6.** Causality __

   Comments: _____

II. *Teacher/instructional language (written or oral)*
   A.   Explanation/direction: (l) Simple _____ Complex _____ Confusing _____

   B.   Use of multiple concepts: _____

   C.   Questions: Form _____   Type _____

   D.   Speaking mode: Length _____   Rate _____

   Comments: _____

III. *Student language (What requisites does the student need?)*
   A.   Comprehension
        Vocabulary: _____

        Syntax (sentence structure): _____
   B.   Production
        Speaking: _____

        Reading: _____

        Writing: _____

   Comments: _____

IV. *Hypotheses:*

   _____

   _____

   _____

   _____

Identification
Name:
Age:
Instructional
   level:
Date:

Subject:

Objective:

Specific
   task:

I. *Language content/concepts*
   A. *Explicit (vocabulary)*   B. *Implicit (concepts/operations)*
      _____   **1.** Classification   **2.** Conservation __
      _____   Sorting   __ **3.** Time   __
      _____   Class inclusion __ **4.** Seriation   __
      _____   Class exclusion __ **5.** Space   __
      _____   Regrouping   __ **6.** Causality   __

   Comments: _____

II. *Teacher/instructional language (written or oral)*
   A. Explanation/direction: (l) Simple _____ Complex _____ Confusing _____

   B. Use of multiple concepts: _____

   C. Questions: Form _____ Type _____

   D. Speaking mode: Length _____ Rate _____

   Comments: _____

III. *Student language (What requisites does the student need?)*
   A. Comprehension
      Vocabulary: _____

      Syntax (sentence structure): _____
   B. Production
      Speaking: _____

      Reading: _____

      Writing: _____

   Comments: _____

IV. *Hypotheses:*

_____

_____

_____

_____

Identification
Name:
Age:
Instructional
   level:
Date:

Subject:

Objective:

Specific
   task:

I. *Language content/concepts*
   A. Explicit (vocabulary)   *B.* *Implicit (concepts/operations)*
   _____   **1.** Classification   **2.** Conservation __
   _____   Sorting   __ **3.** Time   __
   _____   Class inclusion __ **4.** Seriation   __
   _____   Class exclusion __ **5.** Space   __
   _____   Regrouping   __ **6.** Causality   __

   Comments: _____

II. *Teacher/instructional language (written or oral)*
   A. Explanation/direction: (l) Simple _____ Complex _____ Confusing _____

   B. Use of multiple concepts: _____

   C. Questions: Form _____ Type _____

   D. Speaking mode: Length _____ Rate _____

   Comments: _____

III. *Student language (What requisites does the student need?)*
   A. Comprehension
      Vocabulary: _____

      Syntax (sentence structure): _____
   B. Production
      Speaking: _____

      Reading: _____

      Writing: _____

   Comments: _____

IV. *Hypotheses:*
   _____

   _____

   _____

   _____

Analysis of Language Interaction (Mathematics—Practice Exercise 4)

Identification
Name:
Age:
Instructional level:
Date:

Subject:

Objective:

Specific task:

I. Language content/concepts
   A. Explicit (vocabulary)   B.   Implicit (concepts/operations)
   _____
   _____
   _____
   _____
   _____

   1. Classification   **2.** Conservation __
       Sorting   __ **3.** Time   __
       Class inclusion __ **4.** Seriation __
       Class exclusion __ **5.** Space   __
       Regrouping   __ **6.** Causality __

Comments: _____

II. Teacher/instructional language (written or oral)
   A. Explanation/direction: (l) Simple _____ Complex _____ Confusing _____

   B. Use of multiple concepts: _____

   C. Questions: Form _____ Type _____

   D. Speaking mode: Length _____ Rate _____

   Comments: _____

III. Student language (What requisites does the student need?)
   A. Comprehension
      Vocabulary: _____

      Syntax (sentence structure): _____
   B. Production
      Speaking: _____

      Reading: _____

      Writing: _____

   Comments: _____

IV. Hypotheses:
   _____
   _____
   _____
   _____
   _____

Analysis of Language Interaction (Mathematics—Practice Exercise 5)

Identification
Name:
Age:
Instructional
level:
Date:

I. Language content/concepts

A. Explicit (vocabulary)   B. Implicit (concepts/operations)

_____   **1.** Classification   **2.** Conservation ___

_____   Sorting   __ **3.** Time   __

_____   Class inclusion __ **4.** Seriation   __

_____   Class exclusion __ **5.** Space   __

_____   Regrouping   __ **6.** Causality   __

Subject:

Comments: _____

II. Teacher/instructional language (written or oral)

Objective:

A. Explanation/direction: (l) Simple _____ Complex _____ Confusing _____

B. Use of multiple concepts: _____

C. Questions: Form _____ Type _____

D. Speaking mode: Length _____ Rate _____

Comments: _____

III. Student language (What requisites does the student need?)

Specific
task:

A. Comprehension
Vocabulary: _____

Syntax (sentence structure): _____

B. Production
Speaking: _____

Reading: _____

Writing: _____

Comments: _____

IV. Hypotheses:

_____

_____

_____

_____

Practice Exercise 6 (Third Grade)[8]

Objective To solve word problems

Specific Task Multiplication

Ms. Stacey is a reporter for her town's daily newspaper. She is waiting at the train station to interview a state senator. Four trains arrive at the station each hour. How many trains will arrive in 3 hours?

Practice Exercise 7 (Third Grade)[9]
Objective Place value

Specific Task Ordering

Arrange the following numbers in order from greatest to least:
  3245
  4352
  3452
  3524
  4253
  5342
  5234
  2543

Practice Exercise 8

An additional activity to challenge the reader is to analyze the goals and expectations for a specific grade or level. School districts usually have developed a scope and sequence of math goals and objectives for each grade level.

An example from the Madison Metropolitan School District Curriculum Handbook (1981) can be used as a guide.

---

[8] Adapted from Nichols, E., 1978, p. 181.
[9] Adapted from Macmillan, 1976, p. 225.

Identification
Name:
Age:
Instructional
level:
Date:

Subject:

Objective:

Specific task:

I. *Language content/concepts*
   A.   *Explicit (vocabulary)*   *B.*   *Implicit (concepts/operations)*

       _____   **1.** Classification   **2.** Conservation __
       _____   Sorting   __ **3.** Time   __
       _____   Class inclusion __ **4.** Seriation   __
       _____   Class exclusion __ **5.** Space   __
       _____   Regrouping   __ **6.** Causality   __

   Comments: _____

II. *Teacher/instructional language (written or oral)*
   A.   Explanation/direction: (l) Simple _____ Complex _____ Confusing _____

   B.   Use of multiple concepts: _____

   C.   Questions: Form _____ Type _____

   D.   Speaking mode: Length _____ Rate _____

   Comments: _____

III. *Student language (What requisites does the student need?)*
   A.   Comprehension
       Vocabulary: _____

       Syntax (sentence structure): _____
   B.   Production
       Speaking: _____

       Reading: _____

       Writing: _____

   Comments: _____

IV. *Hypotheses:*

   _____

   _____

   _____

   _____

Identification

Name:

Age:

Instructional level:

Date:

Subject:

Objective:

Specific task:

I. Language content/concepts

   A. Explicit (vocabulary)   *B.* Implicit (concepts/operations)

   _____   **1.** Classification   **2.** Conservation __

   _____   Sorting   __ **3.** Time   __

   _____   Class inclusion __ **4.** Seriation   __

   _____   Class exclusion __ **5.** Space   __

   _____   Regrouping   __ **6.** Causality __

   Comments: _____

II. Teacher/instructional language (written or oral)

   A. Explanation/direction: (l) Simple _____ Complex _____ Confusing _____

   B. Use of multiple concepts: _____

   C. Questions: Form _____ Type _____

   D. Speaking mode: Length _____ Rate _____

   Comments: _____

III. Student language (What requisites does the student need?)

   A. Comprehension

      Vocabulary: _____

      Syntax (sentence structure): _____

   B. Production

      Speaking: _____

      Reading: _____

      Writing: _____

   Comments: _____

IV. Hypotheses:

_____

_____

_____

_____

C.A.	Grade level	Cognitive period	Math skills	Concepts/ operations	Instructional (vocabulary)	Math sentences
6	1	Late preoperational (4–7) according to Copeland (1980) during this period the student is developing mathematical concepts which include: Topological space Simple classifications Seriation & ordering Number conservation Length conservation Area conservation	I. Sets 1. Inserts missing sets, such as a set of 3 between a set of 2 and a set of 4 2. Uses physical objects to demonstrate renaming a number 3. Joins sets to define addition 4. Separates sets to define subtraction 5. Selects the number of objects associated with a given number up to 20	I. Sets A. Seriation B. Comparatives C. Class inclusion D. Class exclusion E. Association F. Conservation	*Between, more than,* *join, separate, member, empty set, same, greater than, less than*	Choose the correct set ● is a member of: b a [△ ▲] b [○ ○ / ●] $6 > 5$ or $5 < 6$
			II. Number theory and numeration systems 1. Demonstrates numeral/ number association to 20 2. Is able to sequence a set of numerals through 20 3. Recognizes and uses symbols for equality (=), addition (+), and subtraction (−)	II. A. One-one correspondence B. Seriation C. =, +, −, conservation number, cardinal number	*before, after, next to, all, one, two, three* *equals, addition (plus) subtraction (minus) take away* *Six plus one = seven* *Six and one is seven*	$6 + 1 = 7$ $6 − 1 = 5$
			III. Mathematical sentences and properties 1. Understands the use of +, −, and =	III. Comprehends written symbols		
			IV. Whole number computation 1. Recalls addition facts through sums of 10 2. Is able to add numerals less than 10 3. Recalls subtraction facts through 10 4. Is able to subtract numerals less than 10	IV. Class inclusion Class exclusion	conjunction *and*	$6 + 1 = 7$ (Class inclusion) $6 − 1 = 5$ (Class exclusion)

C.A.	Grade level	Cognitive period	Math skills	Concepts/ operations	Instructional (vocabulary)	Math sentences
			V. Decimals and fractions Demonstrates an understanding of *whole* and *half*	V. Part/whole relationship	Ring shapes that show one half.	
			VI. Geometry Identifies squares, rectangles, circles, triangles, and gives a distinguishing characteristic of each	VI. Spatial, discrimination sorting	Attributes of shapes—round, square, rectangle, long, short, and circle *Put an x on the shapes that are the same.* *Ring the object that has the same shape.*	
			VII. Measurement Is able to order 5 objects by size	VII. Seriation Ordinal number	Complete the pattern △ △ △ ___ Number the pictures from *smallest* to *largest*; *big, bigger, biggest*; and *first, second, third*	
			VIII. Integers			
			IX. Graphing and statistics			

References

Carpenter, T., Corbitt, M. K., Kepner, H., Lindquist, M., and Reys, R. 1981. Results From the Second Mathematics Assessment of the National Assessment of Educational Progress. National Council of Teachers of Mathematics Inc., Reston, VA.

Copeland, R. W. 1974. Diagnostic and Learning Activities in Mathematics for Children. MacMillan, New York.

Copeland, R. W. 1970. How Children Learn Mathematics. MacMillan, New York.

Knight, L., and Hargis, C. H. 1977. Math language ability: its relationship to reading in math. Lang. Arts. 54:423–428.

Lavatelli, C. S. 1973a. Piaget's Theory Applied to an Early Childhood Curriculum. American Science and Engineering Inc., Cambridge.

Lavatelli, Celia S. 1973b. Teachers Guide—Early Childhood Curriculum. American Science and Engineering, Inc., Cambridge.

Lorton, M. 1972. Workjobs. Addison-Wesley Publishing Co., Reading, MA.

MacMillan Mathematics Series N (Teacher's Edition-Level 1) 1976. MacMillan, New York.

Madison Metropolitan School District Curriculum Handbook. 1981. Madison Metropolitan School District, Madison, WI.

Nichols, E. (ed.). 1978. School Mathematics. (Teacher's Edition) Grade 3, Holt, Rinehart, and Winston Inc., New York.

Payne, J. N. 1980. Sense and nonsense about fractions and decimals. Arith. Teach. 27:5–6.

Piaget, J., Inhelder, B., and Szeminska, A. 1966. The Child's Conception of Geometry. Basic Books, Inc., New York.

Russell, D. 1956. Children's Thinking. Blaisdell Publishing Co., MA.

Skypek, D. H. 1981. Teaching Mathematics: Implications from a theory for teaching the language arts. Arith. Teach. 28:13–17.

Suppes, P. et al. 1976. The Random House Mathematics Program (Teacher's Edition-Grade 3), Random House Inc., New York.

Thoburn, T., Forbes, J., and Bechtel, R. 1982a. MacMillan Mathematics (Teacher's Edition-Level 1). MacMillan, New York.

Thoburn, T., Forbes, J., and Bechtel, R. 1982b. MacMillan Mathematics (Teacher's Edition-Level 5). MacMillan, New York.

Williams, Elizabeth, and Shuard, H. 1970. Primary Mathematics Today. Longman Group Ltd London.

Zweng, Marilyn J. 1979. The problem of solving story problems. Arith. Teach. 27:2–3.

Suggested Readings

Carpenter, T. P. et al. 1980. Solving Verbal Problems: Results and Implications From National Assessment. Arith. Teach. 28:8–12.

Earp, Wm. W., and Tanner, F. W. 1980. Mathematics and Language. Arith. Teach. 28:32–34.

Lorton, Mary 1972. Workjobs. Addison-Wesley Publishing Co., Reading, CA.

Peckd, D. M., and Jencks, S. N., Conceptual Issues in the Teaching and Learning of Fractions. J. Res. Math. Educ. 1981, 12:339–348.

Russell, David, 1956. Children's Thinking. Blaisdell Publishing Co., Waltham, MA.

Wadsworth, Barry J. 1978. Piaget for the Classroom Teacher. Longman Publishing Co., New York.

Chapter 8
Reading in the Content Areas (Social Studies and Science)

Social Studies
  Demonstration Example
  Practice Exercises
Science
  Demonstration Example
  Practice Exercises

The development of oral language always has been stressed as a necessary prerequisite to reading. This is true, but an oral language ability does not guarantee reading success. Print is not simply oral language written down. The use of natural oral language consists of false starts, incomplete sentences, repetitions, or the use of single words or phrases to represent sentences. For many children, the introduction to the written language (reading) is their first experience with the formal structure of language, and this may account for their difficulties in comprehension.

Reading skills essentially are divided into two areas—decoding and comprehension. In decoding, phonology plays an important role; in comprehension, syntax and semantics are the important bases (Athey, 1977).

Johnson and Myklebust (1967) suggested that reading is a symbol system twice removed from the reality that it represents. This means that the student must first have concrete, meaningful experiences within his or her environment; next, comprehend and speak the words used in that environment; and finally, learn a written symbol system representing the *experience* and the *spoken word*.

Problems in reading comprehension in the content areas can result from the following:

1. The student's inability to associate meaning (concepts) with oral and written words because of insufficient experiences on the concrete level

2. Oral usage and comprehension problems attributable to the student's inability to understand idioms, inflections, humor, inferences, incongruities, fact versus fantasy, causality, and double function words

3. Reading systems that have complex sentence structure. (Students using only three or four words in a sentence may experience great difficulty in understanding and using the complex written form.)

Reading social studies and science materials utilizes many of the same skills needed in order to read in any other subject area. These skills include the student's understanding of complex sentences and the concept/operations of sequencing and comparing (seriation), classification, space, time, cause and effect, and inference (critical thinking). Students must be able to apply these skills to reading comprehension (Wilson and Hammill, 1982) and interpretation of maps, graphs, tables, and diagrams.

To illustrate some of these concepts/operations that affect comprehension is the following story, which represents a 6.5 reading grade level (Spache, 1963, p. 14). The numbers in the story correspond to the list of skills following the story.

> Elephants are found wild today only in warm regions—in tropical Africa and in India (1). The story was very different 50 thousand years ago (2). Then, two species of the elephant family roamed North America and Europe (1) in numbers.
>
> One of them was the Mastodon. The Mastodon lived in the Eastern Part of our country (1) during the period of the Great Ice Age (2). In the swamps that were formed when (3) the ice disappeared, many of the huge creatures were trapped and killed. We have found some of their skeletons. At a glance, the mastodon must have looked much like (4) the elephants of today, except that it was covered with coarse, woolly hair and its tusks were much larger (4), (5). It was probably heavier (4) than the elephants we know but not taller (4). Its head was flatter and its lower jaw longer (4). Its teeth were not like the teeth of the elephants of today (6).
>
> More than 200 years ago (2) the people of New England (1) found bones of the mastodon when they dug ditches to drain swamps. At first they thought that the bones they found were bones of giant people. When they found teeth that weighed more than four pounds apiece, they decided that the giants were giants indeed (7).

1. Space
2. Historical time
3. Time
4. Comparatives
5. Complex sentence
6. Class inclusion
7. Inference

Social Studies

Table 8.1 shows some examples of concepts/operations inherent in the social studies curricula (Kellman and Nyberg, 1980). It translates curric-

Table 8.1 Concepts/operations in social studies

Curriculum	Concept/ operation
Population Topographical maps	Seriation
Outlining Community helpers Ethnicity Occupations	Classification
B.C.–A.D. Renaissance Revolutionary period	Time (historical)
Maps Graphs Globes Diagrams	Space
Effect of rainfall on agriculture List the reasons for Effect of climate on housing and clothing	Causality

Adapted from Kellman and Nyberg, 1980.

ular content into concept/operations that may affect the student's comprehension of reading in the content areas.

Demonstration Example A (Third Grade)[1]

A lesson on latitude and longitude from a social studies textbook is used here for an analysis of language interaction.

Latitude and Longitude

Vocabulary:

Latitude	Tropic of Cancer
Degree	Tropic of Capricorn
Arctic Circle	Longitude
Antarctic Circle	Prime meridian
	Greenwich

Latitude In order to help us find places on maps, mapmakers use lines of *latitude*. You have already learned about one such line. It is called the *equator*. The equator is halfway between the

---

[1] Loften, 1982, pp. 23–24. Reprinted by permission from: Communities and resources. In: The World and Its People. Copyright © (1982) Silver Burdett Co.

North Pole and the South Pole. *It is a very special line of latitude. It is numbered 0°. All other latitude lines measure distances north or south of the equator.* This distance is measured in *degrees*. The symbol for degrees is °.

Look at the map on the left (see figure at bottom of page). You will see that the city of Minneapolis, Minnesota is located at 45 degrees north latitude (45°). St. Augustine, Florida is located near 30 degrees north latitude (30°N).

In addition to the equator, four other lines of latitude are named. Two of them are the *Arctic Circle* and the *Antarctic Circle*. The Arctic Circle is near the North Pole. The Antarctic Circle is near the South Pole. The coldest parts of the earth are between the Arctic Circle and the North Pole, and between the Antarctic Circle and the South Pole.

The other two named lines of latitude are near the equator. They are the *Tropic of Cancer* and the *Tropic of Capricorn*. The area between these two lines is called the tropics. Most of the warmest parts of the earth are in the tropics. It is hot all year long in most parts of the tropics.

How hot or cold a place is depends a lot on the latitude. The farther north a place is from the equator, the colder it is. The closer a place is to the equator, the hotter it is.

Longitude   Lines of another kind are drawn on maps to help us find places. These are lines of *longitude*. Look at the right-hand map. Longitude lines are drawn from the North Pole to the South Pole. *A special line of longitude is* called the *prime meridian. It is numbered 0°. All other longitude lines measure distances east or west of the prime meridian.* The prime meridian passes through a place in England called *Greenwich*. Half of all longitude lines are west of Greenwich. The other half are east of Greenwich.

Let us find the city of Manaus, Brazil, on the map. Manaus is in the Western Hemisphere. To make it easier to find, you could tell someone that Manaus is at 60° west longitude on the map.

Now find Leningrad, in the Soviet Union. Leningrad is east of the prime meridian. So we say that is at an east longitude. To be even more exact we can say that it is at 30° east longitude.

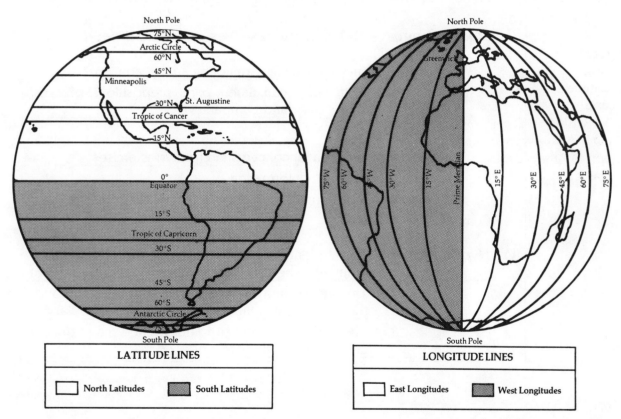

LATITUDE LINES	
☐ North Latitudes	▨ South Latitudes

LONGITUDE LINES	
☐ East Longitudes	▨ West Longitudes

Have pupils draw a large round circle to represent the globe. Tell them to label the North and South poles. Introduce lines of latitude and have pupils draw and label the following lines: equator, Tropic of Cancer, Tropic of Capricorn, Arctic Circle, and Antarctic Circle. Then introduce lines of longitude and have pupils draw and label the prime meridian. Ask: Which lines run in a north-south direction? Which lines run in an east-west direction?

Identification	**I.** *Language content/concepts*
Name:	A. *Explicit (vocabulary)* B. *Implicit (concepts/operations)*
Age: 8	

I. *Language content/concepts*

A. *Explicit (vocabulary)*

latitude	left
longitude	between
degree	year
closer	warmest/colder
near	far/halfway

B. *Implicit (concepts/operations)*

1. Classification		**2.** Conservation	__
Sorting	__	**3.** Time	X
Class inclusion	__	**4.** Seriation	X
Class exclusion	__	**5.** Space	X
Regrouping	__	**6.** Causality	X

Comments: Only the words that express the implicit concepts are listed, e.g., seriation: comparatives (colder, warmest); causality

(depends on distance from equator).

II. *Teacher/instructional language (written or oral)*

A. Explanation/direction: Simple __X__ Complex _____ Confusing _____

B. Use of multiple concepts: _____

C. Questions: Form **what** _____   Type **narrow**

D. Speaking mode: Length _____   Rate _____

Comments: While simple sentences are used, the content is complex.

III. *Student language (What requisites does the student need?)*

A. Comprehension

Vocabulary: Primarily vocabulary denoting spatial concepts

Syntax (sentence structure): constituent parts: prepositional phrases and comparatives.

B. Production:

Speaking: Verbalize spatial concepts in checkup exercises

Reading: Lesson to gain information

Writing: Draw representation of globe and label parts

Comments: _____

IV. *Hypotheses:* **1.** The student may have difficulty in drawing (written language) the representation of longitude and latitude.

2. The student may not be able to comprehend and use the underlying spatial concepts and vocabulary.

3. The structure of the simple sentence may conceal the complexity of the content.

Identification column:

Name:
Age: 8
Instructional level: 3rd grade
Date:

Subject: Social studies

Objective: Geography

Specific task: Latitude and longitude

Checkup

1. What do the lines of latitude measure?

2. What do the lines of longitude measure?

Implications for Instruction

Hypothesis 1 The student may have difficulty drawing the representation of longitude and latitude. The task requires the dealing with part/whole relationships and transferring the student's concept of the globe from three dimensions to two dimensions.

Hypothesis 2 The student may not be able to comprehend and use the underlying spatial concepts and vocabulary. This is critical. The student may not be able to complete the task of locating specific cities by longitude and latitude because he or she does not have the necessary linguistic or conceptual spatial skills. The necessary conceptual skills must emanate from the student's perception of the self in space, which gives rise to the words (linguistic) *left, right, near, between, top, bottom,* and *closer.* Experiences at the concrete level should precede the subsequent academic requirements of representing space in a paper-and-pencil (two-dimension) task.

The students may have difficulty following directions in sentences such as:

"The Arctic Circle is *near* the North Pole."

"The coldest parts of the earth are *between* the Arctic Circle and the North Pole."

"Leningrad is *east* (right) of the prime meridian."

"Minnesota is located at 45° *north* (up or top)."

In this case, intervention could be directed concretely at developing the concept indicated. It is best to utilize the materials of the specific academic task so that the meaning of the concepts in the context can be developed.

Hypothesis 3 The structure of the simple sentence may conceal the complexity of the content. Many textbooks written for the primary-grade level use a simple sentence construction. The objective of using simple sentences is to ensure clarity to facilitate comprehension. However, many simple sentences become difficult for the student to comprehend because of multiple prepositional phrases (some used as a subject) and multiple concepts. In addition, many simple sentences are followed by simple sentences, beginning with the conjunctions *so* and *because.* This syntactical structure has implicit complexity because of the dependent relationship. The use of constituent parts (conjunctions) can turn a simple sentence into a complex one. Intervention strategies should include an analysis of the student's ability to comprehend these constructions. This analysis becomes especially important for special education teachers, who may utilize a variety of textbooks that are written at a high interest and low vocabulary level but contain an implicit complexity of the sentence structures. It is this complexity which may interfere with the student's comprehension.

Practice Exercises

The preceding example illustrates the process of analyzing language interaction in social studies. Analyses of additional examples in social studies would be redundant. It is more advantageous at this point for the reader to be involved in doing the analyses. Examples will be provided with incomplete analyses forms. Remember, there are no right or wrong hypotheses; they must, however, relate to the components of the triad within the specific task (see Chapter 3 on hypotheses formulation).

Practice Exercise 1 (Seventh–Ninth Grades)[2]

The following exercise is analyzed in all three sections of the Analysis of Language Interaction form. The reader should complete the hypotheses.

Relating Cause and Effect American history is often viewed as one long list of unrelated events arranged in the order in which they occurred. But as you know from studying American history up to this point, events do not just happen. There is always a past event or series of events that *causes* a new event to occur. For example, the

[2] Buggey et al., 1982, p. 666. Reprinted by permission from: America! America! (2nd Ed.) by L. Joanne Buggey, Gerald A. Danzer, Charles L. Mitsakos, and C. Frederick Risinger. Copyright © (1982) Scott, Foresman and Co.

Identification	I.	Language content/concepts			
Name:		A. Explicit (vocabulary)	B. Implicit (concepts/operations)		
Age:			**1.** Classification	**2.** Conservation	__
Instructional		Past, present, future	Sorting __	**3.** Time	X
level: 7th–		causes, effects	Class inclusion X	**4.** Seriation	X
9th grade					
Date:		Series of events	Class exclusion __	**5.** Space	__
Subject:		Comments: _____			

Social studies

II. *Teacher/instructional language (written or oral)*
A. Explanation/direction: Simple _____ Complex _____ Confusing _____
B. Use of multiple concepts: _____XX_____

Objective:
To relate
cause and
effect

C. Questions: Form _____ Type _____
D. Speaking mode: Length _____ Rate _____
Comments: Multiple concepts in "make a chart that will show five happen-
ings that help cause this event and five effects of the event.

III. *Student language (What requisites does the student need?)*
A. Comprehension
Vocabulary: Time and seriation words; class inclusion words (all, some)
Syntax (sentence structure): If-then relationship

**Specific
task:**

**Library
research**

B. Production
Speaking: _____

Reading: _____

Writing: 1) Develop chart   or 2) Write a paper

Comments: _____

IV. *Hypotheses:*

_____
_____
_____
_____

Revolutionary War was *caused* by a series of events—the British tax on tea, the Stamp Act, the stationing of British troops in Boston, and the sending of British troops to Concord and Lexington.

The war itself, the *effect* or result of the series of events, in turn affected or caused future events to occur.

History, therefore, is not just a long list of un-related happenings. The fabric of history is a tightly woven combination of past, present, and future.

In this chapter, you have been reading about the cold war. Use your knowledge of this period and reference materials from your library to complete one of the following two activities:

1. Choose one of these events: McCarthy's Anti-Communist campaign, Berlin Airlift, Korean War. Then make a chart that will show five happenings that helped *cause* the event, and five *effects* of the event.

To help you get started, one *cause* of Mc-Carthyism was the Soviet Union's possession of atomic weapons. One *effect* of McCarthyism was blacklisting.

2. Write a one-page paper that will back up the following "theory" of history: "History is like a row of dominoes, push one over and the others will follow after."

Practice Exercise 2 (Fifth Grade)[3]

In this exercise, information is provided in Section I, Language Content/Concepts. The reader should complete the remaining portions of the form and formulate the hypotheses.

Find the answers to these questions:

1. What is meant by the *division of power?*

2. What is meant by the *separation of power?*

3. What is the system of *checks and balances?*

The word *federal* means in a union of individual states. The United States is made up of state governments and a national, or federal, government. The states are tied together by the national government.

Power is divided between the federal government and the 50 state governments. Certain powers are held only by the federal government. These include the power to make war and peace, to mint money, and to control trade between states and with foreign countries. Powers that are not given to the federal government by the Constitution remain with the states. State powers include control of education, marriage, and divorce. Some powers are held by both federal and state governments. These include the powers to tax and borrow money.

The founding fathers feared that any government might become too powerful. To control the power of the federal government, they separated power among three branches in the government. The legislative branch (Congress) makes the laws. The executive branch (President) enforces the laws. The judicial branch (federal courts) helps to interpret the meaning of the laws.

A system of checks and balances. This system makes sure that no single branch of the government gains all the power. Each branch has a way of checking the others. For example:

a. Congress makes the laws, but all bills go to the President before they can go into effect. If the President does not think a bill would be a good law, he may veto it. In this way he can check Congress.

b. A two-thirds majority of Congress may pass a bill over the *disapproval* and veto of the President. Then the bill becomes a law. This is one way that Congress can check the President.

c. The President appoints ambassadors and federal judges. The Senate must give its approval of these appointments. This is another way that Congress can check the President.

d. The Supreme Court may find laws unconstitutional after the laws have been passed and approved. In this way the judicial branch checks both Congress and the President.

e. Congress establishes the federal courts. The President appoints federal judges who must be approved by the Senate. In this way both Congress and the President can check the judicial branch.

Practice Exercise 3 (Fifth Grade)[4]

Test Your Skill Make a time line showing the period from 1850 to 1900. Draw a line lengthwise down the center of a sheet of paper. Let 2 inches represent 10 years. On one side of the line, write in all the big events you studied in Unit 9—the discovery of the Comstock Lode, the Homestead Act, the first long drive, and so on. On the other side, write in events that were going on in the rest of the country. To do this, you will probably have to look back at Units 6, 7, and 8.

---

[3] Abramowitz, 1975, pp. 118–119. From The American Nation: Adventure in Freedom by Jack Abramowitz. Copyright © (1975) Follet Publishing Co. Reprinted by permission from: Allyn and Bacon, Inc.

[4] Buggey et al., 1982, p. 536. Reprinted by permission from: America! America! (2nd Ed.) by L. Joanne Buggey, Gerald A. Danzer, Charles L. Mitsakos, and C. Frederick Risinger. Copyright © (1982) Scott, Foresman and Co.

Analysis of Language Interaction (Social Studies—Practice Exercise 2)

Identification
Name:
Age:
Instructional
   level:
Date:

Subject:

I. Language content/concepts
   A. Explicit (vocabulary)   B.   Implicit (concepts/operations)

system	federal		1. Classification		2. Conservation __
division	state		Sorting	__	3. Time __
separation			Class inclusion	X	4. Seriation __
checks			Class exclusion	X	5. Space __
balances			Regrouping	X	6. Causality X

Comments: _____

Social studies
Objective:
American
   system of
   government

II. Teacher/instructional language (written or oral)
   A. Explanation/direction: Simple _____ Complex _____ Confusing _____

   B. Use of multiple concepts: _____

   C. Questions: Form _____ Type _____

   D. Speaking mode: Length _____ Rate _____

   Comments: _____

Specific
   task:

III. Student language (What requisites does the student need?)
   A. Comprehension
      Vocabulary: _____

      Syntax (sentence structure): _____

Balance of
   power
   B. Production:
      Speaking: _____

      Reading: _____

      Writing: _____

   Comments: _____

IV. Hypotheses:

_____
_____
_____
_____
_____

Cues

1. List the language content/concept skills that the student must bring to the task in order to complete it successfully.

2. Do *not* complete the rest of the summary analysis form.

Science

To understand the cognitive and linguistic demands upon a student in the area of science, consider the following suggestions for developing comprehension, which are found in the teachers' edition of a biology textbook, ninth–twelfth grades (Kaskel et al., 1981, p. 50T).

1. Have students prepare an outline of the chapter. Use the main section headings as Sections I, II, and III. Below each section, use the numbered headings such as 3:1 and 3:2 (*classification* and *seriation*).

2. Have students write sentences by using each of the words provided in the word list (*sentence structure*).

3. Have students look up the plurals of class, genus, kingdom, phylum, and species. A dictionary will be needed (constituent parts/plurals; seriation for alphabetizing)

The textbook continues with the following objectives for the task of classifying living things (p. 51T):

1. To recognize how things are grouped in their everyday lives (identify vocabulary/sorting)

2. To list traits used in grouping some non-living things (attributes)

3. To list reasons for classifying things (causal relation/*why* questions)

4. To devise their own classification system for some objects (*grouping*)

5. To list problems with classifying things (multiple attributes—inclusion versus exclusion)

6. To compare classifications of Linnaeus in grouping living things (seriation/comparatives)

7. To list in order the modern classification groupings (seriation)

8. To learn that the more groups two things have in common, the closer they are related (multiple classification)

9. To describe how things are scientifically named (vocabulary/sentence structure)

10. To find names of living things on a map (sorting)

11. To state reasons scientific names are used instead of common names (critical thinking/vocabulary/sentence structure)

12. To name the three kingdoms in which scientists place living things (classification)

Table 8.2 (Kellman and Nyberg, 1980) translates curricular content into the concept/operations that may affect student comprehension.

Table 8.2 Concepts/operations in science

Curriculum	Concept/operation
Ordering by attribute Comparing Sequencing by size and shape	Seriation
Grouping of organisms and species Attributes of mammals	Classification
Seasons Elapsed time (*Before* and *after*) Change in properties over time	Time
Motion Planets Interstellar space	Space
Reasons for change Hypotheses Prediction	Causality

Identification
Name:
Age:
Instructional level: 7th- 9th grade
Date:
Subject:

Social studies

Objective:

Specific task:

I. *Language content/concepts*
   A. *Explicit (vocabulary)*   B. *Implicit (concepts/operations)*

        _____   **1.** Classification   **2.** Conservation __
        _____   Sorting   __ **3.** Time   __
        _____   Class inclusion __ **4.** Seriation   __

        _____   Class exclusion __ **5.** Space   __
   Comments: _____

II. *Teacher/instructional language (written or oral)*
   A. Explanation/direction: Simple _____ Complex _____ Confusing _____
   B. Use of multiple concepts: _____
   C. Questions: Form _____ Type _____
   D. Speaking mode: Length _____ Rate _____
   Comments: _____

III. *Student language (What requisites does the student need?)*
   A. Comprehension
      Vocabulary: _____
      Syntax (sentence structure): _____
   B. Production
      Speaking: _____

      Reading: _____

      Writing: _____
   Comments: _____

IV. *Hypotheses:*

_____
_____
_____
_____

Demonstration Example B (Fifth Grade)[5]

A lesson on weather, wind direction, and land forms is used for an analysis of language interaction.

Weather, Wind Direction, and Land Forms

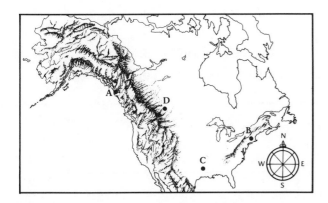

The kind of weather that goes with winds from different directions depends upon many things. At city *A*, for example, an ocean lies to the west. Mountains lie to the east. At *A* a west wind would bring air from a cool ocean surface. So the weather would be cool and damp. An east wind would bring air from dry land and down a mountain. So it would bring warm, dry weather.

Why might an east wind at *B* bring cool, damp weather? Why might a west wind bring drier weather?

A west wind at *A* would bring moisture, perhaps rain, from the ocean. But by the time the air crossed the Rocky Mountains, it would have lost most of its moisture. When it got to *D*, it would probably be dry. A city at *D* would have far different weather from a city at *A*.

A warm sea lies just south of *C*. So, with a south wind, *C* might have warm, damp air, with rain and maybe thunderstorms. But with a south wind, *D* might have only hot, dry weather. There is no warm sea near *D*.

The student is required to answer the following questions (Rockcastle et al., 1980, p. 350). If the student has difficulty, the Summary Analysis of Language Interaction form, which follows the questions, offers some suggestions for intervention.

---

[5] Reprinted by permission from: Rockcastle, V., McKnight, B., Salamon, F., and Schmidt, V. (1980). Earth Science, Grade 7–9. Copyright © (1980) Addison-Wesley Publishing Co., Inc.

The drawing below is a map of North America.

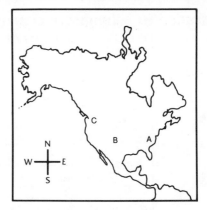

What type of weather might a west wind bring to area *A*?

What type of weather might a west wind bring to area *C*?

What wind direction might bring cold, dry weather to areas *A*, *B*, and *C*?

Which area would probably have the most dry weather?

What would cause this?

Place an *X* on the map in the area where you live.

What type of weather might an east wind bring to your area?

What would cause this?

What type of weather might a south wind bring to your area?

Implications for Instruction   The short text of the lesson consists primarily of simple sentences. Read the text again. What makes the text so difficult? A review reading brings out the problem the student faces in visualizing and verbalizing the effect of *change* in weather based on wind direction and land forms. In addition, the student must deal simultaneously with two directions (reversibility). This could account for the student difficulty expressed in Hypothesis 1, that of demonstrating the representation of spatial relationships.

Intervention strategies could be directed toward making the task more concrete: labeling of the cities on the map instead of using letters; representing the wind current by arrows; using a typologic globe; and pairing relationships—mountain/dry, ocean/wet.

Identification **Name:** **Instructional** **level:** 5th grade **Date:** **Subject:** Science **Objective:** To show how weather is influenced by wind di- rection and land forms **Specific** **task:** To predict probable weather	*I.* **Language content/concepts**

I. Language content/concepts

A. Explicit (vocabulary)   *B. Implicit (concepts/operations)*

east, west, north, south   **1.** Classification _____   **2.** Conservation __

direction   Sorting _____   **3.** Time __

probable   Class inclusion __   **4.** Seriation __

_____   Class exclusion __   **5.** Space   X

_____   Regrouping __   **6.** Causality   X

Comments: _____

II. Teacher/instructional language (written or oral)

A. Explanation/direction: Simple _____ Complex __X__ Confusing _____

B. Use of multiple concepts: _____XX_____

C. Questions: Form why, what, which _____ Type narrow-broad

D. Speaking mode: Length _____ Rate _____

Comments: _____

III. Student language (What requisites does the student need?)

A. Comprehension

Vocabulary: spatial concept words; inferential words (probable)

Syntax (sentence structure): If/then constructions; content of simple sentences

Becomes complex due to conjunctions at beginning of succeeding sentences

B. Production

Speaking: _____

Reading: Reading for information

Writing: Complete worksheet by formulating sentence responses

Comments: The use of "but" at the beginning of sentence denotes negation.

IV. Hypotheses: **1.** The student may have difficulty demonstrating the representation of spatial relationships.

2. The student may have difficulty comprehending the causal relationships represented by sentences beginning with *so* and *but* as well as implicit if-then relationships.

3. The student may have difficulty with the instructional language.

The problem encountered in Hypothesis 2, that of using words such as *so, but* and *if/then* has been discussed in the social studies example.

Similarly, in Hypothesis 3, the problems encountered in causal relationships have been discussed several times. It is encumbent upon the teacher to determine if the student can comprehend and express causal relationships in concrete forms. The expectation of this example is that the student should express causal relationships in an abstract form.

Practice Exercise 1 (Second Grade)[6]

Complete the hypotheses section for the following exercise.

Find the Liquids

1. Which liquid is about to change shape?
2. Which liquid is sour and has a strong odor?
3. Which liquid is sweet?
4. Which liquid is sticky?
5. Which picture does not show a liquid?
6. How are A, B, and C alike?

---

[6] Reprinted by permission from: Houghton Mifflin Science, Grade 2, p. 31. Copyright © (1979).

Practice Exercise 2 (Fourth Grade)[7]

In this exercise, complete the relevant sections of the Analysis of Language Interaction Form.

Activity: Producing Oxygen

What To Use: Elodea plant
Container for water
Test tube
Clock
Hand lens
Water

What To Do

1. Break the growing tip from the Elodea.
2. Place the tip into a test tube. Place it in top first.
3. Fill the test tube with water.
4. Fill the container half-full with water.
5. Cover the top of the test tube with your finger. Turn the test tube upside down into the container. If the plant is giving off oxygen, bubbles will form.
6. Place the container and test tube in a bright light. Wait 15 minutes. Look at the water in the top of the test tube. Look for a bubble of gas in the tube.

---

[7] Sund, 1980, p. 8. Reprinted by permission from: Charles E. Merrill Publishing Co.

Identification
Name:
Age:
Instructional
  level: 2nd
  grade
Date:

Subject:

Science
Objective:
Properties of
matter

**Specific
task:**

Observing
liquids

I.   Language content/concepts

A.   *Explicit (vocabulary)*   B.   *Implicit (concepts/operations)*

liquid	odor		**1.** Classification		**2.** Conservation X
change	sweet		Sorting	X	**3.** Time __
shape	sticky		Class inclusion	X	**4.** Seriation __
sour	not		Class exclusion __		**5.** Space __
strong	alike		Regrouping __		**6.** Causality __

Comments: _____

II.   Teacher/instructional language (written or oral)

A.   Explanation/direction: Simple __X__ Complex _____ Confusing _____
B.   Use of multiple concepts: none _____

C.   Questions: Form **which, how** _____ Type **narrow** ____
D.   Speaking mode: Length _____ Rate _____

Comments: _____

III.   Student language (What requisites does the student need?)

A.   Comprehension
     Vocabulary: **attributes** _____
     Syntax (sentence structure): *how* **question** _____
B.   Production:
     Speaking: **naming objects** _____
     Reading: **attributes of objects** _____
     Writing: _____

Comments: _____

IV.   Hypotheses:

_____
_____
_____
_____
_____

What Did You Learn?

1. Was oxygen given off when the plant was
   first put in the light?

2. What did you observe after 15 minutes?

Using What You Learned

1. Why is the oxygen produced by plants useful to people and animals?

2. How does air pollution affect plants?

Analysis of Language Interaction (Science—Practice Exercise 2)

Identification

Name:

Age:

Instructional level:

Date:

Subject:

Objective:

Specific task:

I. Language content/concepts

A. Explicit (vocabulary)   B. Implicit (concepts/operations)

_____

_____

_____

_____

_____

1. Classification   **2.** Conservation ___
Sorting ___   **3.** Time   ___
Class inclusion ___ **4.** Seriation   ___
Class exclusion ___ **5.** Space   ___
Regrouping ___   **6.** Causality   ___

Comments: _____

II. Teacher/instructional language (written or oral)

A. Explanation/direction: Simple _____ Complex _____ Confusing _____

B. Use of multiple concepts: _____

C. Questions: Form _____ Type _____

D. Speaking mode: Length _____ Rate _____

Comments: _____

III. Student language (What requisites does the student need?)

A. Comprehension

Vocabulary: _____

Syntax (sentence structure): _____

B. Production

Speaking: _____

Reading: _____

Writing: _____

Comments: _____

IV. Hypotheses:

_____

_____

_____

_____

Practice Exercise 3 (Seventh–Ninth Grades)[8]

In this exercise, complete the hypotheses.

Activity: Graphing Stars

a

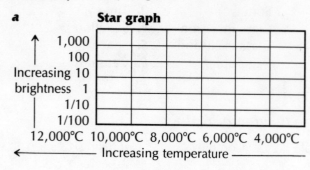

Star graph

1,000
100
Increasing 10
brightness 1
1/10
1/100

12,000°C 10,000°C 8,000°C 6,000°C 4,000°C
← —————— Increasing temperature —————— →

b

Star	Temperature	Brightness	Color
A	3,500	1/10	red
B	13,000	1,000	blue
C	11,000	100	blue
D	3,000	1/10	red
E	4,500	1/10	orange
F	10,000	10	blue
G	4,000	1/10	red
H	6,000	1	yellow
I	7,000	1	green
J	5,000	1/10	red

Purpose To show that graphing the brightness and temperature of stars produces a pattern.

---

[8] Pasachoff et al., 1983, p. 54. Reprinted by permission from: Scott Foresman Earth Science by Jay M. Pasachoff and Timothy M. Cooney. Copyright © (1983) Scott, Foresman and Co.

Materials
Sheet of plain white paper
Cm ruler
Set of colored pencils

Procedure
1. Use the ruler to draw a graph like the sample in *a*. The bottom line is 14 cm long. Vertical lines are 7 cm long and 2 cm apart. Horizontal lines are 1 cm apart.

2. Label the brightness and temperature sides of your graph as in *a*.

3. On your graph, plot the ten sample stars listed in *b*. Make one dot of the proper color for each of the 10 stars. The stars with greater absolute brightness are at the top of the graph.

4. Connect the dots to make a smooth line.

5. Enter a newly studied star on your graph. Its temperature is 3,500° and its brightness is 100. Use the proper color dot.

Analysis

1. How does color relate to a star's position on the graph?

2. What is the name of the line connecting the stars on your graph? (See the graph in 3–4.)

3. What type of stars have you graphed on the line?

4. Why did you select the color you used for the unknown star? What kind of star is it?

Identification	**I.** *Language content/concepts*
Name:	A. *Explicit (vocabulary)* B. *Implicit (concepts/operations)*
Age: 12–14	centimeter, long, a part — 1. Classification ___ 2. Conservation X
Instructional	horizontal, vertical, — Sorting X 3. Time ___
level:	brightness, plot, ___
7th–9th	each of, greater — Class inclusion X 4. Seriation X
grades	absolute, top ___
Date:	temperature, — Class exclusion ___ 5. Space X
	position, select ___
	Regrouping ___ 6. Causality X
Subject:	Comments: comparative relationships; measurement; metric system ___

Science

Objective:
To show
brightness
and tem-
perature of
stars.

II. *Teacher/instructional language (written or oral)*

A. Explanation/direction: Simple __X__ Complex __X__ Confusing _____

B. Use of multiple concepts: _____

C. Questions: Form <u>what, how, why</u> _____ Type <u>narrow/</u>
                                                     <u>broad</u>

D. Speaking mode: Length _____ Rate _____

Comments: _____

Specific
task:

III. *Student language (What requisites does the student need?)*

A. Comprehension
Vocabulary: **Explicit vocabulary representing spatial, comparative, meas-
urment, classification concept/operations**

Syntax (sentence structure): **complex sentences**

Graphing

B. Production:
Speaking: _____

Reading: _____

Writing: **Representing spatial information and comparative relationships,
measurement, classification in a graph form**

Comments: _____

IV. *Hypotheses:*

_____

_____

_____

_____

Summary

The student's success in reading in the content areas, although dependent on his or her decoding skills, is based on comprehension ability. Factors that may affect reading comprehension in the content areas may include:

1. Major sentence structure and the constituent parts

2. Complexity and length of sentence structure

3. Sentences beginning with conjunctions denoting causality

4. Introduction of new vocabulary expressing new concepts versus new vocabulary expressing old concepts

5. How expectations and language of the task match the student's cognitive level

6. The use of multiple concepts in a sentence and/or paragraph

7. The development of concepts in a logical and sequential manner

8. The form and type of instructional questions

9. The teacher's expectation of student's response

10. The instructional use of abstract language

References

Abramowitz, J. 1975. The American Nation: Adventure in Freedom. Follett Publishing Co., Chicago, IL.

Athey, I. 1977. Syntax, semantics and reading. In: Guthrie, John T., (ed.) Cognition, Curriculum and Comprehension. International Reading Assoc., DE.

Buggey, J. 1982. (et al.) America! America! (2nd Edition). Scott Foresman and Co., Glenview, IL.

Getis, A., and Getis, J. 1982. Geography (Teacher's Ed.) Houghton Mifflin and Co., Boston.

Houghton Mifflin 1979. Science, Grade 2. Houghton Mifflin and Co., Boston.

Johnson, D., and Myklebust, M. H. 1967. Learning Disabilities: Educational Principles and Practices. Grune and Stratton, New York.

Kaskel, A., Hummer, P. J., and D. L. 1981. Biology: An Everyday Experience. Charles E. Merrill Publishing Co., Columbus, OH.

Kellman, M., and Nyberg, B. 1980. Piaget and the Curriculum: An Inservice Course for Teachers. Madison Metropolitan School District, Madison, WI.

Loften, R. H. 1982. The World and Its People: Communities and Resources, Social Studies, Grade 3) Silver Burdett Co., IL.

Pasachoff, J., Pasachoff, N., and Cooney, T. 1983. Earth Science, Grade 7–9. Scott Foresman and Co., Glenview, IL.

Rockcastle, V., McKnight, B., Salamon, F., and Schmidt, V. 1980. Science, Level 5, Addison-Wesley Publishing Co., Reading, MS.

Spache, G. 1963. Diagnostic Reading Scales, Reading Level 6.5, McGraw-Hill Book Co., CA. p. 14.

Sund, R., Adams, D., Hackett, J. 1980. Accent on Science (Teachers Ed.), Grade 4. Charles E. Merrill Publishing Co., Columbus, OH.

Wilson, C., and Hammill, C. 1982. Inferencing in comprehension in ninth graders reading geography textbooks. J. Read. 25:424–428, February.

Suggested Readings

Furth, H. 1970. Piaget For Teachers. Prentice-Hall Inc., Englewood Cliffs, N.J.

Goodman, K. S. 1972. Reading: The Key is in the Children's Language. The Reading Teacher, March.

Herber, H. 1970. Teaching Reading in Content Areas. Prentice-Hall Inc., Englewood Cliffs, N.J.

Johnson, D. and Pearson, D. 1978. Teaching Reading Vocabulary. Holt, Rinehart and Winston, Inc., New York.

Pearson, D. P., and Johnson, D. 1972. Teaching Reading Comprehension. Holt, Rinehart and Winston, Inc., New York.

1977. Reading, language and learning. Harvard Educ. Rev. (a special issue) 47, August.

Goodman, Y. (issue ed.) 1982. Instruction in reading comprehension. Top. Learn. and Learn. Disabil. 1, January.

Appendix

The Teacher Language Form[1] measures the *quantity* of teacher/student talk, as well as the *kind* of teacher talk. This recording form depicts the various categories selected from the Amidon-Flanders (1967) profile. With each category, an explanation and description is given as well as procedures for recording information. After a teacher has become familiar in using this modified form, he or she may want to pursue this more fully by referring to the procedures in *The Role Of The Teacher In The Classroom*, (Amidon-Flanders, 1967); *Developing Teacher Competencies*, (Weigand, 1971); and *Classroom Questions* (Sanders, 1966).

The Observation of Teacher Language Form from Madison Public Schools (see Figure A-1) measures the *quantity* of teacher/student talk, as well as the *kind* of teacher talk. It helps the teacher to gain insights into his or her pattern of language influence on the students and to revise language behavior to maximize teacher strategies in order to obtain the desired academic goals.

Teacher Language Categories

The following outline depicts the various categories of the observation form:

Indirect Influence (Types of Statements That Increase Student's Freedom to Respond)

1. Praise or reinforcement of student's feelings and ideas
   a. Accepting students' feelings, both positive and negative
   b. Verbal and nonverbal acceptance (verbalizing; clarifying; supporting students' feelings, gestures, smiles, etc.; and indicating acceptance of feelings
   c. Accepting, reinforcing, clarifying, restating, and expanding student ideas

---

[1] Adapted from Amidon and Flanders (1967).

Direct Influence (Types of Statements That Restrict Student's Response)

2. Criticism of student's feelings, ideas, behavior, etc.
   a. Sarcasm
   b. Negative statements
   c. Cutting off a student
   d. Ignoring students' feelings, verbalization, and behavior
   e. Frowning, glaring, negative gestures, etc.
   f. Questioning students' behavior and response
3. Feedback
   a. Commenting
   b. Expansion of student's utterances
4. Explanations
   a. Explanation of the task, activity
   b. Giving facts, opinions
   c. Lecturing
   d. Rhetorical questions
5. Directions
   a. Commands
   b. Orders requiring a response from the student

(NOTE: Observer may want to differentiate task directions from management directions)

6. Questions
   a. Narrow: Questions requiring yes/no responses, very short responses (few words), identification, and responses that can be easily predicted
   b. Broad: Open-ended questions with less predictable responses; require longer responses, problem solving, and hypothesis testing

Student Talk/Response

7. Student response:
   a. Verbal: Any verbal response to directions, questions, explanation, and encouragement from the teacher.
   b. Nonverbal: Any nonverbal response to directions, questions, explanation, and encouragement from the teacher.

Observation of Teacher Language

Form 3

Sampling time: **51 Seconds**   Name of recorder: **Eunice**   Activity: **Sequencing**

Name: **Susan**   Date: **5/10/75**   Page number: **1**

		Total	Percentage
1. Praise and/or reinforcement		1	5.5
2. Criticism		0	0
3. Feedback		0	0
4. Explanations		3	16.0
5. Directions 　a. Task (T) 　b. Management (M)		4	22.0
6. Questions 　a. Narrow (N) 　b. Broad (B)		3	16.0
7. Student response 　a. Verbal (V) 　b. Nonverbal (N)		0	0
8. Student initiation		1	5.5
9. Silence		6	33.0
10. Interruptions and/or confusion		0	0
TOTALS		18	

Activity Notes:

Figure A-1 Observation of Teacher Language Form.

8. Student initiation
   a. Any verbalization initiated by the student.
   b. Student's shifting to expression of own ideas when responding to a question from the teacher.

Other

9. Silence
   a. Pauses, periods of silence during conversation.

   b. A "no response" to direction, question, etc.
10. Interruptions or confusion
   a. Irrelevant interruptions by other teachers, faculty, or students—a break in the interaction.
   b. Noise, distractions, etc., that interfere with communication.

The form in Figure A-1 is used to record observations of teacher language. The categories in the chart correspond to the following definitions, providing a framework for use of the charting form.

Procedures for Charting[2]

1. It would be helpful for an observer other than the teacher to become familiar with the activity of the classroom for approximately 5–10 minutes before beginning to chart. After the observer has become acclimated to the situation, he or she may then begin to chart the interaction. It is recommended that the teacher personally tape (audio or video) a portion of the lesson for charting teacher language.

2. A thorough knowledge of the categories and the definitions is crucial for use of this form for charting teacher/student language interaction. Otherwise, the teacher may become so involved in attempting to determine the category that he or she will lose track of the interaction and recording time.

3. Every 3 seconds, the teacher should record or check the category of interaction just observed. If more than one category occurs during the 3-second interval, then all of the categories used in that interval should be checked and each change in category recorded; if no change occurs within 3 seconds, the previous category should continue to be checked. It is important to keep the tempo as steady as possible, but it is even more important to be accurate. It is recommended that small samples of teacher/student language interaction are first recorded. To improve skill in recording observations and also to improve the reliability of what is recorded, teachers should observe samples of the teacher language behavior (other than their own) with two or three other teachers, and compare their results. Amidon and Flanders (1967) indicated that it takes approximately 6–10 hours of training before becoming fairly adept at recording the observations reliably.

4. Further practice in recording may be obtained by charting the teacher and student talk in the various tapes that have been pro-

duced as part of this in-service training program. This may be necessary to formulate the hypotheses required by the particular training tapes in this in-service program.

5. The teacher must stop recording or checking the categories whenever the classroom activity is changed. When the classroom activities change, indicate this on the form in Figure A-1. Continue recording again when the teacher resumes verbal interaction with one or more students in a task. It would be inappropriate to record various groups working around the classroom, students working in their workbooks, or doing silent reading.

6. The teacher who is observing the teacher/student language interaction must also realize that diverse instructional activities may evoke different types of teacher/student language behavior. For example, a math group in a third-grade classroom is obviously different from "show-and-tell" time, discussion of a story just read, directions for seat work, or the introduction of new words to the students. When the observer begins to analyze and interpret the data on the form, these variations must be kept in mind.

Discussion

Teacher Language Categories 5 and 6, which cover directions and questions, are very important because they affect the student's responses. These categories provide key information regarding the student/teacher interaction. Teachers spend a great deal of time giving directions and asking questions during instructional activities.

There are many ways to chart question types. For the purposes of this book, question types are divided into only two categories—narrow and broad. These were defined in the categories of observation. To identify narrow and broad questions more easily the following chart has been prepared.

Questions (code)

Type	Form
Narrow (N)—predictable, factual, recall	*what, who, where, is, which, can, do*

---

[2] Adapted from Amidon and Flanders (1967).

Broad (B)—comprehension, *why, how,*
generalization, *what if, could*
inference *it be*

Many times, a teacher asks a series of questions in order to obtain the desired response from the student. In this attempt at clarification, he or she may indeed confuse the student because the teacher asked inappropriate questions or used the wrong question form in the first place. Both question type and question form are being considered here. Question type refers to the level of thinking (narrow or broad) demanded from the student: recalling facts, naming places, identifying, or a *yes* or *no* reply comprise a lower level of thinking. Forming a generalization, making an inference, or relating cause and effect comprise a higher level of thinking.

Similarly, the form of the question will affect the student's response. The form refers to the "wh" word being used in the question. However, this may be incorrectly expressed. The question word *what*, for instance, can be used in both narrow and broad questions:

1. *What* are the boys doing?

2. *What if* the boys would do that?

The difference in the question form, then, depends upon the words that follow the "wh" word. In charting, teachers must listen to both the entire question and the response that is required before recording the type as broad or narrow.

It is very important to note that broad questions are not necessarily better than narrow questions. It depends upon the academic task, the teacher's expectations or objectives for that task, and the language level of the students. Therefore, the teacher may use broad questions in one situation and narrow questions in another. If the teacher is aware of his or her objectives, he or she will have realistic expectations of the students.

Clarification

1. Ultimatums, directions such as "sit down"; counting, etc., are considered directions rather than criticism. Criticism (such as ignoring a student's feelings or verbalization behavior) does not refer to behavior modification techniques.

2. When the students are given an independent workbook assignment, the activity is ended and charting is discontinued. When the teacher engages in a group activity with two or more students, any interruption by a student's asking a question is marked "S," indicating student interruption. If, on the other hand, the teacher gets up during an activity to check papers or control disruptions, this is marked "T," indicating teacher interruption. In other words, a group teaching session should be considered an enclosed teaching unit, and any interruptions (by teacher or student) is charted. This prevails also when the students are doing a short writing segment in response to a direction. The activity is considered finished when an assignment of some length is given.

3. When a teacher uses the individual approach exclusively for his or her teaching method, his or her activity with each student is considered as an interaction. Each teaching segment should be charted as a separate activity, even though it may be of very short duration. Again, the same criteria prevail as in the section above. Interruptions by either student or teacher during the small segment should be charted.

4. Students' questions are considered student initiations when charting.

5. When a student is called on by name, it should be charted as a question.

6. Indicate starting and finishing times for each teaching activity.

Analysis

After the teacher has completed charting, he or she must then develop a description of the observation. There are several ways to describe the interaction between student and teacher. These procedures have been adapted from Amidon and Flanders (1967).

1. Count the total number of checks in all of the categories (which may include several pages of Teacher Language Form). In the 51-second sample there were a total of 18 checks.

2. Compute the percentage of checks in each of the categories by dividing each of the category totals (1 through 10) by the total number of checks of all categories for that particular observation. This computation gives the proportion of total interaction in the task observed for each category (last column in Figure A-1). Following are the percentages for this sample:

Praise or reinforcement	5.5%
Criticism	0%
Feedback	0%
Explanations	16%
Directions	22%
Questions	16%
Student response	0%
Student initiation	5.5%
Silence	33%
Interruptions or confusions	0%

3. Determine the percentage of total teacher talk that falls in each category by dividing the total for each category (1 through 6) by the sum of those six categories. This provides us with the pattern of interaction that the teacher has used with a group of students. Following are the percentages for this sample:

Praise or reinforcement	9%
Criticism	0%
Feedback	0%
Explanations	27%
Directions	36%
Questions	27%

4. Use the same procedure to determine the percentage of total student talk that falls in each category by dividing the total of each category (7 and 8) by the sum of these two categories. For this sample:

Student response	0%
Student initiation	100%

5. Find the total percentage of teacher talk by dividing the total number of checks in categories 1 through 6 by the total number of checks in all of the categories. For this sample:

Teacher talk	61%

6. Find the percentage of student talk by dividing the total number of checks in categories 7 and 8 by the total number of checks in all the categories. For this sample:

Student talk	5%

7. Find the percentage of silence and interruptions, categories 9 and 10, by dividing the total number of checks in each category by the total number of checks in all categories. For this sample:

Silence	33%

8. After completing the computations, further analysis of categories 6 and 7 may be desired. In category 6, percentages of narrow and broad questions can be determined by totaling the number of narrow questions (Ns) and dividing by the total number of questions. The same procedure would be used for figuring out the percentages for broad questions (Bs). The same method may be applied to category 7 (student response).

This type of computation provides the teacher with information concerning the quality and quantity of teacher and student talk. It is important to remember that the modification of the Amidon and Flanders (1967) system as used here is only an initial step in helping the teacher become aware of how his or her language may influence the responses of the student. A detailed explanation of computing multiple interactions is presented in *The Role of the Teacher in the Classroom* by Amidon and Flanders (1971).

Considerable time should be taken to chart the videotape on teacher language in order to become thoroughly familiar with the procedures before trying to use these tools to analyze the language interaction in math and reading. A suggested preliminary step is for the teacher to audiotape a 5–10 minute sample of his or her interaction with one or a group of students before using the teacher language forms.

As the teacher listens to the tape in private, he or she should try to become aware of:

1. The rate of speech (too fast, too slow)

2. The number of questions asked

3. The number of directions given

4. The approximate amount of teacher talk versus student talk

The purpose of this preliminary listening activity is to develop listening skills regarding a teacher's own language behavior. In order to develop listening skills, it is best to listen for one of the above items at a time. This may require the teacher to listen to the same tape several times.

Summary

Skills in listening and charting a teacher's own language develop over time. Remember, the authors' objective is to help the teacher become aware of his or her own language. Teachers cannot make assumptions about their own language behavior until they collect the data by observing and charting.

References

Amidon, J., and Flanders, N. 1967. The Role of a Teacher in the Classroom. Assn. for Productive Teaching, Inc., Minneapolis.

Cole, R. A., and Williams, D. M. 1973. Pupil response to teacher questions: Cognitive level, length, and syntax. Educ. Read. Res. Suppl., Nov: 142–145.

Cunningham, R. 1971. Developing question asking skills. In: N. J. Weigand (ed.), Developing Teacher Competencies. Prentice-Hall, Inc., Englewood Cliffs, NJ.

Sanders, N. 1966. Classroom Questions: What Kinds? Harper and Row, New York.

Weigand, J. (ed.). 1971. Developing Teacher Competencies. Prentice-Hall, Inc., Englewood Cliffs, NJ.

Glossary

causality A concept which implies a cause-and-effect relation between two phenomena.

classification A strategy for organization based on the principle of grouping and regrouping (similarities and differences).

class inclusion Items belonging together based on single or multiple criterion.

class exclusion Items that do *not* belong together because the items do not meet the characteristics of the single or multiple criterion.

multiple classification To group objects into various subgroups depending on a specific or multiple criterion.

numerical classification Establishes relationships forming the basis of sets resulting in the development of number sequences.

nonnumerical classification Establishes relationships providing a framework for logical thinking.

cognitive development Process of learning and knowing which progresses from sensorimotor, preoperational, concrete operations to formal operations.

conservation The ability to perceive that certain attributes of an object are constant, even though they change in appearance.

constituent parts Parts of speech.

critical thinking Involves evaluation of information and requires accumulations of information to hypothesize solutions to problems.

ecological Refers to the environment in which students function and the interactions of persons within the environment.

expanded triad A schematic representation depicting the many interactions within and between each language component of the basic triad.

explicit concepts Refers to the use of concept words (vocabulary) in instructional tasks.

hypothesis A question or implied question to be answered by collecting further information.

implicit concepts Refers to the underlying concept/operations in an instructional task.

interaction Reciprocal action or influence.

language content/concepts Refers to the meaning or substance of the words to be used in communication. Language content/concept can be represented in nonverbal and verbal forms and underlies all academic knowledge.

morphology Smallest unit of meaning which may be combined to form words. Examples include tenses, plurals, possessives, and comparatives.

phonology Refers to the sound system of a language.

pragmatics Use of language in the context in which it occurs. In this book, the use of language is in the context of academic learning.

questions

broad questions Elicit a higher level of response involving generalizations, comprehension, and inference.

narrow questions Elicit factual, predictable and recall responses that contain 1–3 words.

memory questions Require students to repeat or recognize information previously presented to them.

translation questions Require students to change information into a different symbolic form.

interpretation questions Require students to discover relationships.

application questions Require students to solve a problem in a life situation.

analysis questions Require students to take apart information and make relations by discovering hidden meaning or reading between the lines.

synthesis questions Require students to do imaginative thinking in solving a problem.

reversibility Ability to perceive order from more than one direction (increasing and decreasing size, height, gradation of color and textures, and qualities).

semantics Refers to meaning of language or the knowledge that the speaker must have in order to understand sentences and relate them to his or her knowledge of the world.

seriation Ordering and relationship of objects.

set A collection of any kind of things which belong together based on a single or multiple criteria.

space Perceptual (what we perceive through our senses); representational (what the mind reconstructs).

student language Refers to the comprehension, production, and function of language used by the student in instructional tasks.

syntax Word order and sentence complexity.

teacher language The oral and written language used by the teacher as well as written language of curriculum in an instructional task.

temporal Refers to time; temporal concepts can be in order (sequence) and duration (the interval between two events).

triad A schematic representation depicting the interaction of teacher language, student language, and language content/concepts interacting in specific tasks.

Index

Academic tasks, *see* Instructional tasks
Addition, 11, 12, 24
Adjectives, in student language, 73
Adverbs, in student language, 73
Alphabetizing, spatial development for, 29
Analysis of language interaction, *see* Language interaction analysis
Analysis questions, in teacher language, 56
Application questions, in teacher language, 56
Assessment, *see* Language interaction analysis
Association, mathematics skills requiring, 108
Audiotaping, recording teacher language by, 54

Borrowing, in subtraction, 87–91
Broad questions, 52–53, 131, 132

Causality, *see* Language content/concepts
Charting, recording teacher language by, 55, 131

Classification, *see* Language content/concepts
Class inclusion
in classification learning, 22
mathematics skills requiring, 108
Cognition, language and, 20–21
see also Cognitive development
Cognitive checklists, for language content/concepts, 21, 35–45
Cognitive development
concrete operational stage, 21
causality and, 31, 44–45
classification and, 22, 35
conservation and, 24, 36
seriation and, 28, 40–41
spatial development and, 29
time and, 37–38, 39
formal operational stage, 21
causality and, 31, 45
classification and, 22, 35
conservation and, 36
seriation and, 28, 41
spatial development and, 43
time and, 38
language related to, 20
mathematics skills and, 108
preoperational stage, early, 21
causality and, 31, 44
classification and, 35
conservation and, 36
seriation and, 27–28, 40
spatial development and, 29, 42

time and, 37
preoperational stage, late, 21
causality and, 31, 44
classification and, 35
conservation and, 24, 36
mathematics and, 108
seriation and, 28, 40
spatial development and, 29, 42–43
time and, 37, 38
sensorimotor stage, 20–21
causality and, 44
spatial development and, 29, 42
time and, 37
Cognitive questions, 53
Communication unit, 69
Comparatives
mathematics skills requiring, 84, 108
in student language, 70, 71, 72
Complex sentences, 66, 68–69
Compound sentences, 68, 69
Comprehension, student language and, 66–67
see also Reading comprehension
Concepts, *see* Language content/concepts
Concrete operational stage, *see* Cognitive development
Conjunctions, in student language, 72, 73
Conservation, *see* Language content/concepts

concepts
Constituent parts, in student language, 70
Content, *see* Language content/concepts
Content areas, *see* Language arts; Mathematics; Science; Social studies
Context, language in, 6–7
Creative thinking, classification skills in, 24
Critical thinking, 31–32
mathematics requiring, 83
Curricular units, language interaction analysis performance and, 14

Decimals, 98, 109
Directions, in teacher language, 52
Distance, development of concept of, 25–26

Early preoperational stage, *see* Cognitive development
Ecological assessment, 7
Environment, 7
Euclidean geometric space, 28, 29
Evaluation questions, in teacher language, 56

Expanded triad, 14–15
student language in, 63, 64
teacher language in, 51
Explanation, in teacher language, 52
Explicit skills, in instructional task, 19–20
Explicit use, of language, 71
Explicit vocabulary, 20

Formal operational stage, *see* Cognitive development
Fractions, 96–98, 109

Geometry, 109
Euclidean geometric space, 28, 29
spatial development for, 30
Graphic collections, in classification learning, 22
Graphing, 109

Historical perspective, development of concept of, 26
How questions, in student language, 73
Hypotheses, 11
formulating, 13, 14
intervention based on, 12–13, 14
on mathematics
fractions, 97, 98
place value, 92, 93, 94, 95, 96
sets/matching, 86–87
subtraction/borrowing, 89, 90–91

on science, 121, 122, 123
on social studies, 114, 115
on spatial development, 30
on time manipulation, 27

Implicit concepts/operations, *see* Language content/concepts
Implicit skills, in instructional task, 19–20
Implicit use, of language, 71
Instructional language, *see* Teacher language
Instructional mode, of teacher language, 51–53
Instructional tasks
explicit skills in, 19, 20
implicit skills in, 19, 20
language content/concepts in, 10
language interaction within specific, 9–10
story problems and, 11–13
student language in, 10
teacher language in, 10
Integers, 109